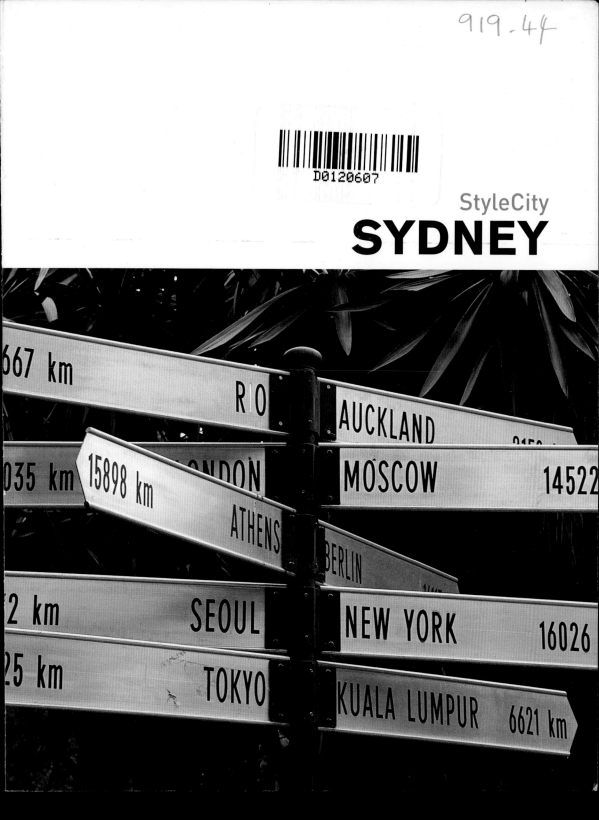

StyleCity
SYDNEY

StyleCity

SYDNEY

With over 400 colour photographs and 8 maps

WITHDRAWN

WITHDRAWN

Contents

Street Wise

Style Traveller

Series concept and editor: Lucas Dietrich
Jacket and book design: Grade Design Consultants
Original design and map concept: The Senate
Maps: Peter Bull

Research and texts: Simon Richmond
Specially commissioned photography by
Anthony Webb.

First published in the United Kingdom in 2004 by
Thames & Hudson Ltd, 181A High Holborn,
London WC1V 7QX

www.thamesandhudson.com

British Library Cataloguing-in-Publication Data
A catalogue record for this book is available from the
British Library

ISBN 0-500-21011-X

Printed in China

How to Use This Guide

The book features two principal sections: **Street Wise** and **Style Traveller**.

Street Wise, which is arranged by neighbourhood, features areas that can be covered in a day (and night) on foot and includes a variety of locations – cafés, shops, restaurants, museums, performance spaces, bars – that capture local flavour or are lesser-known destinations.

The establishments in the **Style Traveller** section represent the city's best and most characteristic locations – 'worth a detour' – and feature hotels (**sleep**), restaurants (**eat**), cafés and bars (**drink**), boutiques and shops (**shop**) and getaways (**retreat**).

Each location is shown as a circled number on the relevant neighbourhood map, which is intended to provide a rough idea of location and proximity to major sights and landmarks rather than precise position. Locations in each neighbourhood are presented sequentially by map number. Each entry in the **Style Traveller** has two numbers: the top one refers to the page number of the neighbourhood map on which it appears; the second number is its location.

For example, the visitor might begin by selecting a hotel from the **Style Traveller** section. Upon arrival, **Street Wise** might lead him to the best joint for coffee before guiding him to a house-museum nearby. After lunch he might go to find a special jewelry store listed in the **shop** section. For a memorable dining experience, he might consult his neighbourhood section to find the nearest restaurant crossreferenced to **eat** in Style Traveller.

Street addresses are given in each entry, and complete information – including email and web addresses – is listed in the alphabetical **contact** section. Travel and contact details for the destinations in **retreat** are given at the end of **contact**.

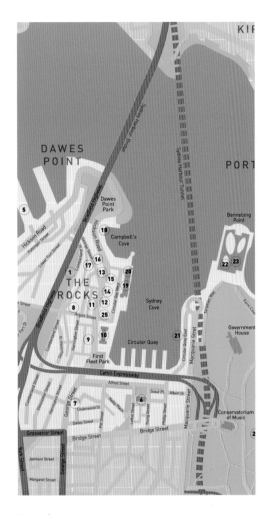

Legend

(2)	Location
	Museums, sights
	Gardens, squares
(M)	Monorail stops
	Streets

SYDNEY

With all the insouciant swagger of a supermodel, Sydney strides on the world catwalk, a confident beauty, flaunting the off-white sails of the Opera House and the sweeping steel girders of the Harbour Bridge, adornments to the justly celebrated crinkle-cut harbour. The city reflects the style of its residents — youthful and bronzed, wearing the sexiest of swimwear and appealing to every sexual persuasion. One wonders how they do it, especially when there are so many delicious dining and drinking opportunities — Sydney is the culinary capital of the southern hemisphere and a place to party like it's perpetually 1999.

Built as a prison, and for over a century considered little more than a parochial backwater at the far end of the Empire, Sydney began to blossom in the run up to its 1988 bicentenary. By the turn of the millennium its time had come, and during the 2000 Olympics Sydney finally shed any remaining cultural prejudices and showed the world exactly what the city was made of. Sydneysiders rejoiced that, at last, their city was recognized for exactly what it is: a damn good place to live.

Blessed with magnificent natural attributes — the harbour, the beaches, an abundance of parkland — Sydney is, in the words of David Williamson, its foremost playwright, the Emerald City. The Eora people who lived here long before the Europeans arrived in 1788 appreciated this. Then, as now, to truly enjoy Sydney you need to be outdoors. The tree-shaded inner suburbs are best covered on foot and some of the prime stretches of harbour and ocean foreshore are woven through with public footpaths, providing views that Sydneysiders will pay through the nose for if glimpsed from a piece of real estate.

There are plenty of other cities with beautiful harbours, lovely beaches and a fun-filled approach to life — Hong Kong and Rio de Janeiro come to mind. What sets Sydney apart, according to Peter Carey, is the sandstone that is the city's 'DNA'. You'll find it everywhere; the honey brown colour and rough hewn texture is as evocative of the city as the leathery, tanned skin of the stalwarts at Bondi's Iceberg swimming pool. Sydney's architecture is a curious, unique mixture. Alongside many Art-Déco beauties stand high-concept contemporary structures such as Renzo Piano's Aurora Place or Harry Siedler's Horizon apartments, not to mention Jørn Utzon's Sydney Opera House (p. 25). Then there is the regal Victoriana of its most prominent civic buildings and the homely grace of the gentrified workmen's terraces and cottages of the eastern suburbs and inner west. At times you could be in the northern English city of Manchester, at others Los Angeles.

Although not a huge city in terms of population (around four million), Sydney is a sprawling one, covering 1,800 square kilometres from the foothills of the Blue Mountains to the west to stunning national parks in both the north and south. It's a fiercely tribal city, too, with fracture lines running north–south and east–west: residents of Paddington seldom stray across the harbour to Mosman and Manly, and those from Vaucluse consider the inner-west suburbs to be a different country (and vice versa).

For all the things that divide Sydney, though, there are plenty that bring it together. The city is home to around 140 nationalities, a multicultural centre that finds its finest expression a dynamic, innovative dining scene. There are few other cities where you can eat so well, across so many different types of cuisine, in such a variety of locations – from a slick temple to gastronomy to fish and chips at the beach.

It's not only in food that Sydney's style credentials are gaining respect in the wider world. As Australia's premier city, Sydney draws artistic talent not only from across the country but over the whole region. Japan's Akira Isogawa (p. 169), New Zealand's Collette Dinnigan (p. 160), and Vietnam's Alistair Trung (p. 19), among others, have joined with local designers behind up-and-coming Australian labels, such as Sass & Bide, tsubi, Michelle Jank and Zimmermann (p. 163), to put Sydney on the international fashion map.

Apart from spawning a plethora of reality TV shows (2003's *The Block* gripped the nation with its blow-by-blow account of how eight yuppies renovated four Bondi apartments), Sydney residents' principal obsession with property has fuelled a parallel fascination with interior design. Zen minimalism, antique flourishes or beach shack-chic – whatever look you want for your home, you can get it in Sydney.

'Is it *really* world class?' pondered Jan Morris in her affectionate biography of Sydney. On all the available evidence – from the classic Sydney of the postcard to the offbeat, quirky, charming, rougish and larrikin elements of one of the world's youngest and most competitive cities – like her you'll conclude that Sydney is indeed a winner.

Street Wise

The Rocks • Millers Point • Circular Quay • CBD • Darling Harbour • Pyrmont • Haymarket • Woolloomooloo • Potts Point • Darlinghurst • Surry Hills • Waterloo • Paddington • Woollahra • Double Bay • Rose Bay • Vaucluse • Watsons Bay • Bondi • Bronte • Clovelly • Inner West Suburbs •

The Rocks
Millers Point
Circular Quay

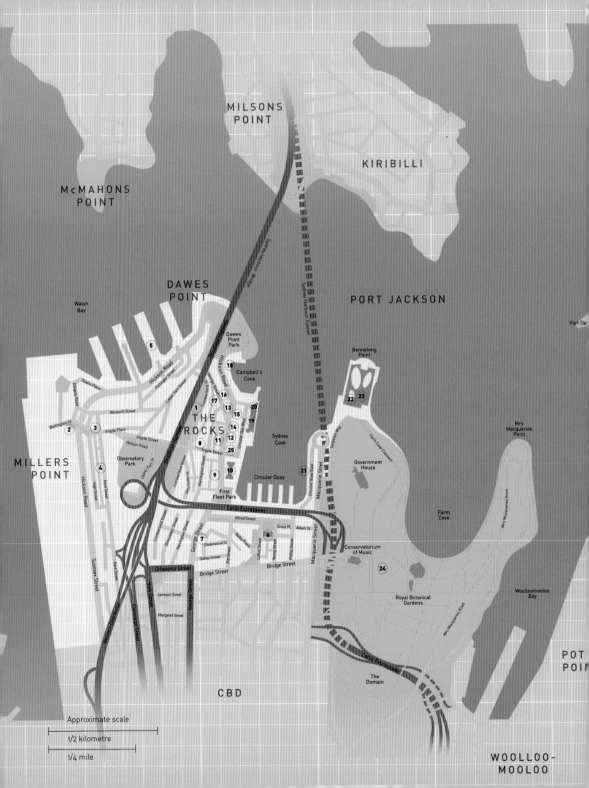

MILSONS
POINT

KIRIBILLI

McMAHONS
POINT

Fort De

DAWES
POINT

PORT JACKSON

Walsh
Bay

Dawes
Point Park

⑤

Bennelong
Point

Campbell's
Cove

Mrs
Macquaries
Point

Windmill Street

⑱

②   ③

⑯
① ⑰ ⑬   ⑳
    ⑮   ⑲
  ⑭

THE
ROCKS

Sydney Cove

Government
House

Farm Cove Crescent

MILLERS
POINT

④

Observatory
Park

⑧ ⑪ ⑫
    ㉕

Argyle Street

⑨   ⑩

②①

Farm
Cove

First
Fleet Park

Circular Quay

Conservatorium
of Music

㉒ ㉓

Woolloomooloo
Bay

⑦

⑥

Alfred Street

Scout Pt.   Albert St

Bridge Street

㉔

Royal Botanical
Gardens

Grosvenor Street

Bridge Street

POT
POIN

Cahill Expressway

CBD

The
Domain

WOOLLOO-
MOOLOO

Approximate scale

1/2 kilometre

1/4 mile

Big international sporting events temporarily shift the focus of Sydney towards its geographical centre at Homebush (site of the Olympic stadia), but at any other time, everyone knows that the city's true heart lies in the dress circle of suburbs radiating from Circular Quay. Landing place of the First Fleet in 1788 and now a commuter hub and recreational magnet for tourists and locals, Circular Quay, along with the adjacent areas of the Rocks and Millers Point, for all its familiarity as a clichéd image of Sydney, never loses its impact. The twin icons of the Harbour Bridge and the Opera House stand like sentinels on either side of Sydney Cove, while the distinctive cream-and-green painted ferries chug in and out of the harbour, which — combined with a breezily blue sky — creates a dazzling view.

Everyone seems to have an opinion about the area: the architect of the Opera House Jørn Utzon stomped off in 1966 swearing never to return. He hasn't, but is helping in the long-overdue redesign of the Opera House's interior. During the 1970s, when the violent slums and nasty stench associated with the Rocks were replaced by shops, souvenir stalls and the aroma of roasted coffee beans, there were those who claimed the area had been robbed of its character and charm. But visitors and Sydneysiders flock here to poke around its quirky boutiques and galleries, shop at the weekend markets or sink an ale at one of its many heritage pubs. The rumpus that greeted the development of East Circular Quay has been quietly forgotten (p. 22), as has the wacky plan to stick a giant structure over the Museum of Contemporary Art (p. 19). One significant grumble that refuses to die down, however, is over the Cahill Expressway, which slices across the quay above the railway station. Everyone would prefer it to be buried underground but, with other cross-city tunnelling projects currently underway, this is unlikely to happen for quite some time.

Attention is currently focused on the rejuvenation of the previously derelict wharves along Millers Point on the west side of the Rocks. In former Bond Stores 2 and 3, the Sydney Theatre Company has opened a new theatre (p. 17) while, opposite, multi-million dollar waterside apartments have been snapped up by Sydney's movers and shakers — in stark contrast to the public housing up on the crest of the Rocks. This area, around Argyle Place and the grassy knoll of Observatory Hill, is the Rocks at its most charming and serene. It feels a world away from the crowds at Circular Quay with its ferries, buses, buskers and tourists licking ice creams, slurping oysters and snapping away at the whole glorious scene.

A VIEW FROM THE BRIDGE

1 The Harbour Bridge & BridgeClimb

5 Cumberland Street

The pageant that celebrated the opening of the world's largest (but not longest) steel arch bridge on 19 March 1932 was a foretaste of all future harbour-based cavalcades. The $20 million bridge, which took 1400 workers nine years to construct, is the focus of many celebrations, its vast arched span doubling as a platform for spectacular firework launches and light displays. Crossing the harbour at one of its narrowest points, the bridge, nicknamed the Coathanger, was designed by Dorman Long & Co of England to the specifications of chief engineer Dr John Bradfield. It has eight traffic lanes and two railways – remarkable foresight given that at the time people were still travelling in horse and cart. Down the west side is a cycleway, on the east a footpath affords glimpses of the Opera House; it's best to start walking from the Milsons Point end and head towards Circular Quay. From the top of the museum on the bridge's history located in the southeastern pylon you can get good views, but undoubtedly the best come from climbing the bridge itself. Although clambering up the girders was done unofficially in the past, since 1998 BridgeClimb has made it a safe, informative and hugely enjoyable three-and-a-half-hour experience. After donning a grey boiler suit and being issued with a communication device (so you can hear the leaders commentary) and safety harnesses, the climb starts from the Cumberland Street end and climaxes at the apex of the arch, 134 metres above the harbour. Climbs depart every 10 minutes, rain or shine, from dawn to dusk – the ones timed to coincide with sunset are the most popular slots, for which you will have to book well in advance. Short of a flight in a seaplane, this is the most spectacular view you will have of Sydney and its beautiful harbour.

THERE SHE SAILS

2 Palisade

BOUTIQUE BREWERY

3 The Lord Nelson Brewery Hotel

THE GRAND DAME

4 The Observatory Hotel

5 Sydney Theatre Company & The Wharf

Pier 4/5 & 22 Hickson Road, Walsh Bay

After years of neglect, the recent development of the old wharves at Walsh Bay into sleek contemporary apartments and penthouses has injected new life into the area, as has the opening of the Sydney Theatre Company's $40 million, 850-seat theatre at 22 Hickson Road, a space it shares with the Australian Ballet and the Sydney Dance Company. The city's premier theatrical company's main headquarters remains across the road at Pier 4/5, one of the four timber structures dating from 1914 that jut 200 metres into Walsh Bay, which houses two of the Sydney Theatre Company's performance stages and spaces used by the Sydney Dance Theatre and the indigenous dance group Bangarra Dance Theatre. At the end of the massive structure, with wonderful 180-degree views of the harbour, is the theatre's bar and the excellent Wharf restaurant. Part owner Tim Pak Poy of Claude's fame (p. 138) has worked with chef Aaron Ross to create a modern Australian menu as appealing as the restaurant's serene location.

QUAYSIDE BALCONY

6 Café Sydney

Level 5, Customs House, 31 Alfred Street

While the grand sandstone Customs House dating from 1885 undergoes a transformation from an office and gallery space into the new City of Sydney library, the rooftop tenant Café Sydney happily remains in business. The spacious balcony with its prime, central position overlooking Circular Quay is the big draw, but the darkly sophisticated interior illuminated by Dinosaur Designs' glowing resin light blocks is also appealing, particularly on Friday nights when there's live jazz or funk music. This is not fine dining, but it's hardly food for slouches either; the menu offers a wide range of fresh seafood and dishes cooked in woks, or in their woodfired and tandoori ovens. Sydney interior-design gurus Burley Katon Halliday have been working on the new lounge area, a 40-seat addition to the intimate bar. The new library downstairs will specialize in reference and history books as well as traveller information. There will be a café and bar, and there are also plans to screen films and hold exhibitions.

NATURE'S FIREWORKS
7 Opal Fields

MEDITERRASIAN PLAYGROUND
8 Argyle Stores
18–24 Argyle Street
• bel mondo
• RoKit
• Helen Kaminski
• Alistair Trung

The former Argyle Bond Stores, built between 1826 and 1881, is one of the more successful heritage renovations in the Rocks. Constructed around a cobbled courtyard, the four-storey brick warehouses with exposed beams have an appealing atmosphere that encourages you to explore. On the top floor is bel mondo, the once-classic restaurant that has survived the departure of big name chef Steve Manfredi mainly because of its magnificent location with glimpses of the Harbour Bridge. Perfectly suited to the retro surroundings is the vintage clothing collection of RoKit. You can also pick up one of Helen Kaminski's distinctive straw sun hats here. Best of all, though, is the fusion fashion of Alistair Trung at his atelier-like space or 'playground', as he calls it. Saigon-born Trung brings a southeast-Asian flair and Mediterranean sophistication to his clothing that won't give women a nervous breakdown. His designs refuse to be pigeonholed, for example a scarf can become a decorative collar or headband, or even a top, depending on your mood and creativity. His use and contrast of fabrics is inspirational, combining mud silk from China and cotton from Guatemala, raw leather and silk georgette, or a fabulous 1950s silk grey graphic print from Milan.

STAR PERFORMER
9 Rockpool

130

THE SHOCK OF THE NEW
10 Museum of Contemporary Art
140 George Street

A couple of years ago Sydneysiders were shocked at the city's plans to develop the site and fund the museum by building a giant, partially transparent structure around the Museum of Contemporary Art, housed in the old Maritime Services Board Building, a striking Art Déco–style building dating from the 1950s. Dubbed the 'coffee table' (a corollary to the notorious 'toaster' on East Circular Quay), the plan was dumped amid a public furore that persuaded the state government to find the money needed to keep the museum, the only one in Australia dedicated to contemporary art, afloat. The drama seemed apt for a gallery dedicated to shaking up complacent approaches to art. The basis of the museum's outstanding collection was the bequest to Sydney University by art collector John Power in the 1940s. Today the museum offers a changing programme of exhibitions, including some of the most interesting and internationally well-known modern Australian artists, as well as works by Andy Warhol, David Hockney and Roy Lichtenstein. The stylishly experimental film, photography and video art of Tracey Moffatt has been displayed here as have the amazingly life-like sculptures of Ron Mueck, Howard Arkley's photographs and Rosalie Gascoigne's multimedia installations.

THE BUSH OUTFITTER
11 R. M. Williams
71 George Street

It is hard to believe that the footwear and clothing of stockmen and cattledrovers of the Australian outback would become a fashion statement for sophisticated urbanites, but that's exactly what has happened to R. M. Williams's merchandise. Exemplary materials and production methods married with elegant, classic design are a major part of the appeal, along with the Australian love of outdoor life and respect for battlers such as Reginald Murray Williams, who first made boots in the far outback of south Australia during the Great Depression, and whose company grew into an international chain. When he died in November 2003 he was afforded a state funeral. The Longhorn brand of elastic-sided leather boots are Australian design at its utilitarian best, and can be purchased here and at R. M.'s other stores around the city.

KING OF THAI
12 Sailors Thai & Sailors Thai Canteen

OBJECT OF DESIRE
13 Object Store

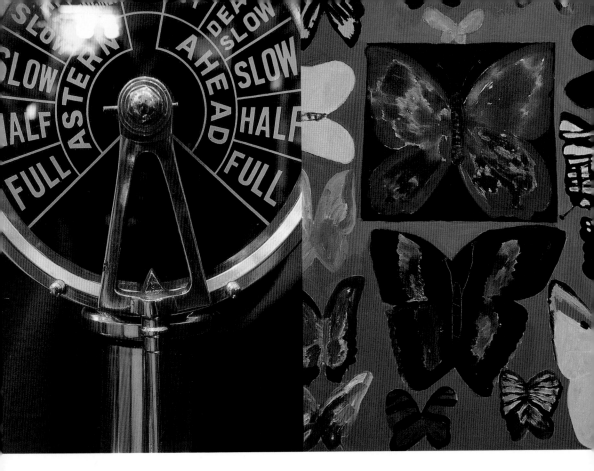

NAUTICAL CURIOS
14 Bottom of the Harbour Antiques
104 George Street

This old curiosity shop with a maritime bent seems like a microcosm of the eclectic authenticity and fakery of the Rocks precincts. Amid all the kitsch nautical reproductions and rag bag collection of Burmese puppets, Lenin pendants and purses made from cane toads, you'll find some items of genuine interest. The brass ship clocks make handsome timepieces and the heavy metal diving helmets from the 1940s and Portuguese and Dutch cannons are real conversation pieces not to mention serious collectors' items. More than likely, though, your eye will be caught by the ranks of jolly sea salts: brightly painted original characters carved from timber.

ARTIST AT WORK
15 Ken Done Gallery
1 Hickson Road

Ken Done's paintings are distinctly redolent of Sydney – its searing bright light, its lush harbour location, its hedonistic lifestyle. The giant colour-saturated canvases appear like exotic flowers amid the exposed woodwork structure of his gallery housed in a former government building. There's a shop selling prints and books and some of the clothing, accessories and homewares created by Done's wife Judy. A wider selection can be found down the road at 123 George Street as well as at outlets in the Queen Victoria Building (p. 33) and across the harbour in Mosman, not far from Done's idyllic waterside home at Chinaman's Beach.

CONTEMPORARY CRAFTS

16 Australian Image Craft & Telopea Gallery Craft

Metcalf Arcade, 80–88 George Street, shop 2

The Society of Arts and Crafts of New South Wales has always taken its work seriously: when the society started in 1906 members were fined if they failed to attend a meeting or didn't exhibit work. The fortunes of the society have waxed and waned, but since 1974 they have found a permanent home in the Metcalf Arcade where members' work is displayed in two spaces: Australian Image Craft and the Telopea Gallery Craft. The former displays larger pieces of work, including wall hangings, rugs and prints, while the latter specializes in gold and silver jewelry, glass and ceramics. You'll often find some intriguing pieces here, maybe not as cutting edge as at the Object Store (p. 170) but still of interest. And since society members staff the galleries you may even get to chat to the artist about his or her work.

DIGERIDOOS AND DAMASK

17 Rocks Market

George & Playfair Streets

Launched in 1991, the weekend arts and crafts street market at the northern end of George and Playfair Streets is a popular place to seek out quirky and stylish gifts. The emphasis is on Australiana – from framed vintage tourism posters of Sydney, koala puppets and mini surfboard clocks to boomerangs, digeridoos and lacquered crocodile jaws. It's worth hunting through the 150 stalls under and around the sail-like cream canopies spanning the road for some of the more unusual souvenirs. Wood artist Peter Stroud creates giant platters and bowls out of Australian hardwoods, such as Red River Gum; Eden Park Designs mount romantic, antique-style prints on square blocks; while Druid Designer Gear offer sculptures inspired by bushranger Ned Kelly's trademark iron mask. With live music drifting out of the Mercantile Hotel, the atmosphere is festive and fun.

18 harbourkitchen&bar

Park Hyatt Hotel, 7 Hickson Road

Opposite the Opera House, the Park Hyatt Hotel snakes around Campbell's Cove, offering all residents a glorious view of the non-stop proceedings of the harbour. If you're not a guest, you can still take a ringside seat on the action at the hotel's harbourkitchen&bar. The sleek dining room has floor-to-ceiling windows and a relaxed, spacious bar area – a great spot to watch the Opera House change colour in the fading evening light with a drink in hand. Anthony Musarra's Mediterranean-influenced food is worth hanging around for: try his gorgonzola tart with prosciutto and slow-roasted pears or prawn ravioli with taramasalata.

BON VOYAGE

19 Overseas Passenger Terminal, Circular Quay West

- Cruise
- Wildfire
- Ember
- Opium
- Doyles at the Quay

The Overseas Passenger Terminal, where some of the world's largest cruise liners berth when they sail into Sydney Harbour, was substantially upgraded for the Bicentenary in 1988. The steel-and-glass structure with a turret at the north end is also the home of several restaurants and bars, among which Quay, on the first floor of the turret, is the best. At the south end the hard-drinking crowd are entertained by the gently glowing kinetic light box behind the bar at Cruise, which changes colours like a chameleon. Next door is the more appealing Ember, a cosy, warmly decorated Art Déco–style bar that provides a stark contrast to its gargantuan sibling Wildfire, the Australian creation of American celebrity chef Mark Miller. This dazzling space seats 300 over two levels, with a frenetic 10-metre-long open kitchen, contemporary chandeliers and a huge wine 'cellar' rising the height of the building. The extensive menu includes house specialities cooked in their wood-fired ovens: pizzas and Brazilian–style churrasco that feature a gut-busting variety of meats and seafood.

The management of Ember and Wildfire has recently taken over the neighbouring modern Asian-influenced restaurant, Opium. Designed by Misho Vasiljevich (a former student of Pritzker Prize winning Australian architect Glenn Murcutt), the vast and theatrical cardboard sculpture covering one wall remains the most interesting thing about the space. If you don't care for the interiors, then you can dine or drink outside the trio of Wildfire venues. If you want to see both the Opera House and the Harbour Bridge, then there's nothing for it but to take a seat at Doyles, the Circular Quay outpost of Sydney's most famous purveyors of fish and chips (see also p. 78).

MOD-OZ CLASSIC

20 Quay

TOASTING THE TOASTER

21 East Circular Quay

1-7 Macquarie Street
- Aria
- Aqua Luna
- ECQ
- Bridge Bar
- The Dendy

The development of East Circular Quay in the run up to the Millennium was controversial. When the 1960s office buildings that had been on the site were demolished a view was opened up from the Botanic Gardens through to the Rocks, but was blocked again by the squat apartment buildings popularly dubbed the 'toaster'. When the area opened in 1999, though, the fuss died down as Sydney discovered the appeal of the broad paved promenade and shady colonnade with boutiques, restaurants and bars. Sydney foodies awarded top marks to the mod-Oz Aria and Italian Aqua Luna, both beautifully seductive places to dine, the latter having double-whammy views of the Opera House and Bridge and a popular ground floor bar with tables spilling out onto the promenade. For more drinks in chic surroundings, the elevated Bridge Bar and ECQ in the Quay Grand Hotel fit the bill. At the heart of the complex is the arty Dendy cinema, the very model of a contemporary picturehouse for the chattering classes.

22 Guillaume at Bennelong Bar

MISTRESS OF THE POINT

23 Sydney Opera House
Bennelong Point

Designed by Jørn Utzon, a Danish architect who had never visited the city, Sydney's most recognizable landmark is nothing short of one of the wonders of the modern world. It took 14 years, $102 million and many engineering headaches to turn the blueprint of this extraordinary creation on Bennelong Point into reality. Nobody doubts that the time, money and dramas were ultimately justified by the beautiful building with its graceful, sail-like roofs – a worthy reply to the Harbour Bridge opposite. This monument to high culture is a democratic place, reflecting the all-inclusive ethos of the city and country. The programme of events and shows covers a broad spectrum from symphonies in the Concert Hall to house music and multimedia shows in the Studio. The grand steps at the front of the building are regularly used as stadium seating for outdoor events, such as the free street-theatre performances that are a key element of January's Sydney Festival.

Even if you're not attending a performance or taking one of the backstage tours, it's well worth getting up close to this intricately constructed building to enjoy the texture of the roof tiles and the wonderful sense of space it conjures. Thirty years on from its debut a major refurbishment of the interior is underway, and it's being supervised by Utzon, who is yet to visit his masterpiece and, most likely, never will. He bares no hard feelings though. 'What matters to me,' said the Pritzker Prize winning architect, 'is that the people of Sydney love it.'

BEAUTIFUL BLOOMS

24 Royal Botanical Gardens
Mrs Macquaries Road

A naturally beautiful foil to the man-made majesty of the Opera House, the Royal Botanical Gardens wrap around Farm Cove and can be accessed from the gate next to the Man O'War Jetty. Established by Governor Macquarie in 1816, the gardens are Australia's oldest scientific institution and home to an outstanding collection of local and exotic flora and interesting fauna, such as possums and a colony of bats whose nightly dusk flight from the gardens towards Centennial Park (p. 69) is one of Sydney's most incredible natural sights. A stroll through the gardens always turns up something fascinating: view rare and threatened specimens such as the Wollemi Pine, thought extinct until rediscovered in the Blue Mountains in 1994, or sniff the aromas of the herb garden. Alternatively, you could just laze on a picnic blanket in the shade of a spreading fig tree or visit Government House, the official residence of the governor of New South Wales. Exotic plants can be seen in the Sydney Tropical Centre, consisting of two Louvre-like glasshouses, the Pyramid and the Arc, while the National Herbarium of New South Wales has around one million dried specimens, including ones collected during James Cook's visit to Botany Bay in 1770.

ISLAND LIFE

25 Cadman's Cottage & Fort Denison
110 George Street

Although Elizabeth Farm in the city's western suburb of Parramatta is a few years its senior, Cadman's Cottage, dating from 1816, comfortably takes the title for the oldest dwelling in central Sydney. Named after convict-made-good John Cadman (transported in 1798 for horse stealing) the compact sandstone cottage now houses the information centre for Sydney Harbour National Park and is the place to book tours to some of the harbour's islands. One of the best trips is Fort Denison, the defensive Martello Tower, originally used as a prison for re-offenders. (It's nickname was Pinchgut because of the austerity diet forced on those inmates lucky enough not be hanged.) Visitors now are given a far heartier welcome at the café in the 19th-century garrison where they can breakfast or lunch on the likes of Tasmanian smoked-salmon frittata or blue-swimmer-crab lasagne while watching the ferries and boats on the harbour.

CBD
Darling Harbour
Pyrmont
Haymarket

It may be known as the Central Business District (CBD) but, thanks to the construction of several residential towers in recent years and the restaurants, bars and clubs that followed, there's a whole lot more going on here than brokering multi-million dollar deals or greasing the wheels of commerce. An area that was once dead during the evenings and weekends now pumps with action, a process that will continue as even more people swap a house in the suburbs for an apartment in the city.

Stretching south from Circular Quay towards Central Station, the CBD is bounded to the west by Darling Harbour and the peninsula of Pyrmont and Ultimo, and to the east by the Botanic Gardens and the Domain. It's an area dominated by high rises on narrow, sometimes twisting, streets that follow the contours of the land. Although much has been destroyed, prime examples of Victorian architecture provide a link to colonial Sydney. Take a turn through the Queen Victoria Building or Strand Arcade (both p. 33), rather than pedestrianized Pitt Street shopping mall, to experience the best of the CBD's consumer possibilities.

A more friendly CBD was created in the run up to the 2000 Olympics, with wider footpaths and improved street furniture, starting with the beautification of Macquarie Street where some of the city's grandest public buildings are, including the State Library, Parliament House, Sydney Hospital, the former Mint and Hyde Park Barracks. The Museum of Sydney (p. 30) and the reopening of the old GPO building (p. 31) followed, combining heritage preservation with commercially viable buildings.

Modern architecture is well represented, from the sensuous curves of Renzo Piano's Aurora Place on Macquarie Street to snazzy King Street Wharf, designed by Cox, Richardson & Crone Associates, which – along with the appealing Cockle Bay Wharf – has swung attention back towards Darling Harbour. Most distinctive of all is the soaring golden pinnacle of the AMP Tower on Market Street, locally known as Centrepoint after the shopping mall from which it ascends. The 305-metre tower is one of the city's highest observation points and currently marks the city's commercial heart, although this could change when the long-running World Square development (a 35-storey residential tower bounded by George, Liverpool, Pitt and Goulburn Streets) is completed, making the area south of Town Hall and north of Central Station a new centre of downtown Sydney. The likely redevelopment of the Carlton and United brewery along Broadway, immediately west of Central Station, will also contribute to the growing gentrification of nearby Ultimo and Chippendale.

DECONSTRUCTING SYDNEY

1 Museum of Sydney

Corner of Bridge and Phillip Streets

Old and modern Sydney meet at the Museum of Sydney, built on the site of the first Government House, which was demolished in 1846, and was a parking lot for decades before the original building's foundations were uncovered in 1980. As part of the approval for the soaring, sharp-edged Governor Philip Tower and adjacent Governor Macquarie Tower, the highly contemporary museum was built. The sandstone façade rises from a rough-hewn base to smooth upper blocks, mirroring the development of the city. Inside and outside the history of the area is revealed in a series of state-of-the-art displays. The Edge of the Trees sculpture on the plaza beside the museum's entrance is a collaboration between Aboriginal and non-Aboriginal artists, combining elements of both cultures' experiences of the city. There is a good bookshop and café, and the museum is the starting point for Sydney architecture walks.

CITY SLICKER

2 Establishment

112

ELEGANCE REVISITED

3 Est.

131

CLUB AFRICANA

4 Hemmesphere

152

LET'S GO ROUND AGAIN

5 The Summit & Orbit

Australia Square, 264 George Street

When Harry Seidler's Australia Square building opened in 1964 it boasted the world's highest revolving restaurant. Following a 2001: A Space Odyssey–style refit in 1998, the Summit restaurant and Orbit bar are back in groovy business, spinning customers through a dazzling 360-degree panorama of the city. The menu also harks back four decades, including such classics as prawn cocktail, oysters kilpatrick and duck à l'orange, as well as bombe Alaska. Slip into one of the retro swivel chairs in Orbit and enjoy a mandarin vodka, shagadelic cocktail, slurpy toffee-apple daiquiri, or order a Martini shaken, not stirred.

MILE-HIGH CLUB

6 Forty One

Chifley Tower, 2 Chifley Square

Restaurant toilets are not places you would usually want to linger, but you'll be tempted to take your time in the ones at Forty One, which have fabulous views of the city. Situated on level 41 of the Chifley Tower (named after former Australian Prime Minister Ben Chifley – it's him smoking a pipe in the giant steel cut-out sculpture in the square below), this high-class domain of chef Dietmar Sawyere offers carefully crafted, award-winning food in a private club-like setting. There's always an inventive vegetarian menu and an encyclopaedic wine list. Courteous waiters run up and down the Titanic–style swirling staircase linking the two levels, delivering dishes such as wild barramundi with Chinese chive and crabmeat dumplings in XO sauce or sweet chocolate truffle cake.

GENERAL REVIVAL

7 No. 1 Martin Place / GPO

- Prime
- Post
- Sosumi

James Barnet's General Post Office (GPO) was once the most significant building in Sydney, its grand colonnade and Italianate clock tower symbolizing British rule. Crowds gathered around the boards that announced ships arriving with mail from the mother country. Following a long period of neglect, the building was revived in the late 1990s when two new tower blocks (one housing the Westin Hotel) were built behind it. Known by its address, No. 1 Martin Place, the restoration retained not only the splendid façade but also the beautifully decorated postal hall dating from 1927 and a magnificent central staircase.

The basement hosts a collection of restaurants, a bar and a small food hall modelled on the one at Harrods in London. Some of the best dry-aged, choice cuts of steak in the city can be devoured at the cellar-like Prime, accompanied by a choice of rich gravy, red wine jus, béarnaise sauce or a selection of mustards. There's more of a seafood slant to the crowd-pleasing, mod-Oz menu at Post, a brightly lit space with plush banquette seating. If you want to be in the middle of it all, pull up a seat beside the conveyor-belt food bar of Sosumi – one of the better *kaiten-zushi* (revolving sushi) restaurants in the city. As well as the usual tuna, salmon and squid topped varieties, they do excellent hand rolls – try the scallop and fish roe combo.

The Strand Arcade, built in 1891, cuts an elegant, terrazzo-paved swathe from George Street to Pitt Street, rising up three floors towards the vaulted glass ceiling. On the ground floor Strand Hatters is the place to pick up classic Australian headgear, including Akubra, Helen Kaminski and lightweight panama hats. There is a branch of the Scandinavian interior-design shop Funkis (p. 81), while Coco Nobué offers very feminine, Asian-inspired fashion. The next level provides a gallery of designer fashion, kicking off with the eclectic fabrics and intricate textures of Alannah Hill's clothes and continuing with the cool threads of Bettina Liano and London-born Wayne Cooper, as well as outlets for Lisa Ho (p. 70) and Zimmermann (p. 163). Take a turn around the lace iron balcony to discover Dinosaur Designs (p. 175) and Love & Hatred: local designer Giovanni D'Ercole's unique contemporary jewelry collection that combines medieval and modern styles. Well cut business suits and shirts for the hip executive about town are provided by Michael Hislop. Nip into Luxe on the second floor for a mix of contemporary fashions, including the latest designer jeans and T-shirts, before finally collapsing at Ichi-Ban Boshi, which serves some of the tastiest and most authentic bowls of Japanese–style noodles in the city.

When the State Theatre, designed by Stuart Doyle and Henry White, opened in 1929 it was hailed the 'Empire's greatest theatre'. Seldom used as a picture palace today, the building remains a glittering homage to the glory days of Hollywood. The Gothic-meets-Art-Déco interior is a riot of crimson velvet, gilt, rococo statutory and a mammoth marble staircase sweeping up towards the four-tonne Koh-I-Nor cut-crystal chandelier, the second largest in the world. The 2000-seat auditorium is now principally used for pop concerts and stage productions, but for two weeks every June the celluloid ghosts of the past return as the theatre becomes home to the Sydney Film Festival, one of the longest-running movie festivals in the world.

Filling an entire city block bounded by George, Market, York and Druitt Streets, the Queen Victoria Building (QVB) was designed by George McRae and completed in 1898. Replacing the original Sydney markets, it is an elaborate Romanesque monument designed to resemble a Byzantine palace and – at a cost of $86 million – was restored to its original grandeur in the 1980s. From the intricately designed tiled floors to the enormous stained glass windows and multi-domed, copper-clad roof, the QVB is a veritable shopping temple, with over 200 outlets over four levels. It's worth taking one of the twice daily tours to discover some of its fascinating corners and details, such as the 23-carat gold coated Great Australian Clock with its series of 15 dioramas and the Royal Automated Clock showing scenes from English history.

Herringbone, on the ground floor, makes fine quality shirts and accessories for men and women, while Oroton is the Australian Louis Vuitton, selling their own stylish leather bags and luggage. For videos, DVDs, books and CDs relating to top Australian TV shows drop by the ABC shop on level one. Above it is Quadrivium, one the CBD's better galleries, showcasing contemporary decorative arts including ceramics, jewelry and glass. At the north end of the building you can go up one more level to the starkly white thetearoom, an appropriately grand and usually quiet place to take tea or enjoy lunch. Use the original lifts to go up and walk down the circular cast-iron staircase. There are plans to give the building a startling makeover using a bold Victorian colour scheme, replacing the central escalators with less obtrusive ones and reinstating a staircase.

ONLY THE BEST
12 David Jones

161

MADE IN AUSTRALIA
13 Gowings

165

MARITIME PLAYGROUND
14 Darling Harbour
- Sydney Aquarium
- Australia National Maritime Museum
- Gavala Aboriginal Art
- Chinta Ria...Temple of Love
- Coast
- Cargo Bar

The development of Darling Harbour into the 'people's place' was part of the New South Wales government's bicentenary programme of city beautification projects. A once derelict goods site is now home to two of Sydney's best tourist attractions – the Aquarium and the Australian Maritime Museum. The pedestrian Pyrmont Bridge links these Philip Cox-designed buildings and separates the southern half of the harbour, with its IMAX cinema and serene Chinese Garden, from its mouth into the main harbour. The gargantuan Harbourside shopping complex, which runs down the west side, is mainly notable for Gavala, Sydney's only entirely Aborigine-owned and -operated art and crafts gallery, which also has an education and lecture programme to introduce visitors to indigenous arts, crafts, dance and music.

Despite the presence of the hugely popular and ugly Star City casino to the north in Pyrmont, this side of the harbour has never really taken off other than with tourists. (An exception is the monthly Saturday morning growers' market in front of Star City).

The east-side developments of the wharves have been much more successful with locals. The multi-tiered structures of Cockle Bay uses sandstone and recycled timbers while Kings Street is all glass and steel – both host many restaurants and watering-holes that have become party-time magnets for the hoards of office workers from the CBD. At Cockle Bay a four-metre-tall Buddha welcomes diners to the silk padded, octagonal Chinta Ria...Temple of Love where you can enjoy traditional Malaysian dishes, such as beef rendang, nasi goreng and chicken laksa, as well as modern interpretations like the snap-fried prawns stuffed with minced prawns, herbs and vegetables. Incense, a lotus pond, temple arch and a breezy wooden balcony complete the Asia-in-Australia look. Next door, along the roof terrace, Coast is making a go of a large space where several other high profile restaurants have floundered. The dining room is as elegant as their globally influenced contemporary food, including spice-rubbed Muscovy duck and tartare of ocean trout. Over in King Street Wharf, there's the super stylish Bungalow 8 and the popular Cargo Bar, which serves gourmet pizza.

ROYAL APPROVAL
15 The Loft

154

NATIVE AUSTRALIAN
16 Edna's Table

133

SEAFOOD GALORE
17 Sydney Fish Market
Corner of Pyrmont Bridge Road & Bank Street

The remarkably vibrant Sydney Fish Market is the largest seafood market outside of Japan, trading 15 million kilograms of fish and shellfish a year. Every day except Christmas Day from 5.30 am, around 170 buyers purchase 65 tonnes of seafood. All of it is so incredibly fresh that there are no lingering smells as you wander the stalls piled high with oysters, prawns, crabs and over 100 different species of fish, as well as practically everything else you could need, from spices to fresh fruit, vegetables and bakery goods. The attached Seafood Cooking School has a regular roster of classes where the city's top chefs demonstrate how to get the best out of the ingredients on sale. If you can't wait to eat, there's an excellent sushi bar, takeaway fish and chips and several restaurants with outdoor tables overlooking Blackwattle Bay.

PERFECT PROVIDORE
18 Simon Johnson
181 Harris Street

Simon Johnson is the patron saint of Sydney foodies, and the man to whom practically every chef worth their Australian salt flakes turns to when they need a specific ingredient or inspiration for a new dish. His Woollahra store might be the epitome of chic but this dark, barn-like space is his main Sydney outlet, stocking one of the city's finest range of gourmet foods. Choose from an incredible range of olive oils, olives, cheeses, Mariage Frères teas, Belgium chocolates and other luxury foods, as well as simple, elegant Italian homewares. The staff are knowledgable, but if you want to learn more of how to use their fabulous provisions grab a programme for the series of talks given here by some of Australia's most respected food writers and chefs.

OENOPHILE'S DREAM
19 Ultimo Wine Centre
99 Jones Street

If you're looking for a specific vintage of Penfold's Grange or any other top Australian wine, this is the place to come. John Osbeiston is Sydney's, if not Australia's, top wine merchant, offering an unparalleled range of wines from around the world, including all major vineyards and many rarely found bottles and vintages. Although they specialize in imported wines, which account for around 65 per cent of their range, the Australian selection is notable for its emphasis on quality rather than price. Wines such as Rockford from South Australia's Barossa Valley or Bass Phillip from Gippsland in Victoria are good examples of this – fine individual wines that you'd be hard pressed to find anywhere else. They also stock an extensive range of accessories, including antique corkscrews and wine-related books.

HANDS ON EDUCATION
20 Powerhouse Museum
500 Harris Street

The latest and greatest in Australian design – from cars to high-tech fabrics and household items – can be found at the Powerhouse Museum. Occupying the old Ultimo Power Station, this is one of Australia's largest and most fascinating museums, home to over 380,000 items covering transport of all kinds, decorative arts and design and Australian social history. The hands-on Experimentation section on the ground floor is a fun way to learn about science. Other highlights include sections on indigenous Australian dance and music; 20th-century fashion and decorative arts; and the 1930s Art-Déco Kings Cinema where old news reels and feature films are screened.

LATE NIGHT DINING
21 Chinatown
- Chinese Noodle Restaurant, 8 Quay Street
- BBQ King, 18–20 Goulburn Street
- East Ocean, 421–29 Sussex Street
- Gallery 4A, 181–87 Hay Street

Paddy's Market, the small vegetable market that was the original heart of Chinatown, is the still there, nestling beneath the populist shopping mall Market City with its fashion discount outlets and Asian food court. Dixon Street, however, is Chinatown's main artery, festooned with neon, a hive of sizzling woks and furious eating late into the night. The legendary BBQ King on Goulburn Street and the cramped Chinese Noodle Restaurant on Quay Street are Chinatown at its most authentic – both serve delicious, cheap food in utilitarian surroundings. In contrast, the contemporary East Ocean, with entrances on both Dixon and Sussex Streets, heralds a new generation of Chinese restaurants where the ambience of the dining room (in this case imperial red and gold) is considered of equal importance to what's served. It's worth digging around the chaotic shops of Chinatown too, not only for Chinese medicines, herbs and Asian ingredients but also for the latest street fashions from Hong Kong and Japan. For more local creativity there's Gallery 4A where, in a handsomely renovated Victorian building opposite the Capitol Theatre, the Asia–Australia Arts Centre organizes exhibitions of local and overseas artists' work; their aim is to challenge traditional perceptions of Australian identity and culture.

DÉCO DELIGHT
22 Civic
151

LIVING TREASURE
23 Tetsuya's
132

24 Hyde Park
Elizabeth Street

Not nearly as extensive as its London namesake, Hyde Park was once Sydney's racecourse. It now provides a green haven for the city, a place to escape the crowds, to enjoy a game of chess with pensioners or take a romantic evening stroll through its central walkway, the overarching fig trees festooned with twinkling fairy lights. At the Liverpool Street end of the park is the monumental Art-Déco Anzac Memorial, designed by Bruce Dellit and completed in 1934. Soldiers and nurses sculpted by Raynor Hoff hang their head in contemplation around its chiselled perimeter while inside the dome is studded with 120,000 stars, each commemorating an Australian who served in the First World War. Forming a counterpoint at the Macquarie Street end of the park is Francois Sicard's Art-Déco Archibald Fountain, built in honour of the friendship of Australia and France during World War I.

TERRAZZO TREASURE
25 St Mary's Cathedral
St Mary's Road

Hyde Park is surrounded by several of Sydney's most impressive religious buildings, including the Byzantine–style Great Synagogue dating from 1878 and St James' Church, the oldest church in Sydney, originally built in 1824. The most impressive, however, is St Mary's Cathedral. Opened in 1882, the building was only recently completed with the construction of its twin spires, which are best viewed from the plaza by the adjacent Cook and Philip Park aquatic and sports centre. It's not until you are inside the Gothic–style building that you realize its true scale; it is the largest Roman Catholic cathedral in the southern hemisphere and much larger than many in Europe. The vaulted roof is 46 metres high, flooded with glowing light through the amber stained-glass windows. The cathedral's jewel, though, is its crypt, laid with a beautiful terrazzo floor incorporating enamelled Celtic patterns around a series of designs depicting the six days of creation.

DEALER'S CHOICE
26 Bambini Trust Cafe
185 Elizabeth Street

A lot of media deals get done at the elegantly wood-panelled Bambini Trust Cafe, tucked away in the sandstone pillars of the St James Trust building facing onto Hyde Park.

Its position as the smartest Italian restaurant and café on the block next to the ACP magazine empire's building practically makes it their staff canteen. Crisp white table linen highlights the simple, beautifully presented food. Come for an intimate dinner of wild-mushroom and lemon risotto or roast duck with grappa soaked muscatels, a simple lunch of some of Sydney's best pasta, or a cappuccino and biscotti to kick-start the day.

TIE ME UP
27 Rochefort
185 Elizabeth Street

Tucked away on the ground floor of the St James Trust Building is this charming boutique devoted to the art of the necktie run by Shane Rochefort and his sister Lisa. Twice a year Shane designs new patterns and colour schemes for the ties, which he hand stitches from sumptuous silk Jacquard sourced from Como, Italy. Along with traditional stripes, floral and fleur de lys patterns, Rochefort's ties come in abstract designs sampling tapestry, dragon, shell and branch motifs. The quality of Rochefort's ties is not just in the fabric but also in their luxurious design: the six-fold style of tie extends the fabric across the whole blade ensuring that it lies flat against the chest. The perfect finishing touch is an embroidered signature on each one.

UNFUSSY FASHION
28 Calibre
139 Elizabeth Street

The minimalist interior of tiled walls and floor forms a stark backdrop for the equally unflashy but enormously stylish menswear of Calibre, a Melbourne label that has two shops in Sydney (the other is on Oxford Street in Paddington; p. 66). In a city short of smart tailoring for men, Calibre's clothes, designed by Gary Zecevic and Freddie Ryan, stand out for their use of fine and luxurious fabrics and clean, unfussy lines – the silky knitwear, sharp suits and fitted shirts are particularly strong. Their shops also carry accessories by top fashion labels, including Gucci, YSL, Dolce & Gabbana and Costume National.

Woolloomooloo
Potts Point
Darlinghurst

THE
ROCKS

Port Jackson

Mrs
Macquaries
Point

Garden
Island

Government
House

Farm Cove Crescent

Farm
Cove

Mrs Macquaries Road

(1)

CBD

Conservatorium
of Music

Macquarie Street

Royal Botanical
Gardens

Woolloomooloo
Bay

ELIZABETH
BAY

Cahill Expressway

The
Domain

Macquarie Street

St James Road

Art Gallery Road

(5)

Art Gallery
of New
South Wales

Cowper Wharf Road

(3)

(4)

(2)

(14)

(6)

Cowper Wharf Road

St Neot Avenue

Wylde Street

Macleay Street

Challis Avenue

(17)

(16)

(13)

Elizabeth
Bay

POTTS
POINT

(18)

Elizabeth
Point

Billyard Avenue

Macleay
Point

Greenknowe Avenue

Elizabeth Bay Road

Rushcutters
Bay

Prince Albert Road

St Mary's Road

Nicholson St

Bourke Street

Plunkett St

Forbes Street

Griffiths St

Best St

Harmer St

Stephen St

Crown Street

Cathedral Street

McElhone Street

Dowling Street

Brougham Street

Victoria Street

Hughes Street

Tusculum Lane

Manning
Street

(12)

(11)

Orwell Street

Earl Street

Springfield Ave

Macleay Street

(15)

(9)

(8)

(7)

WOOLLOO-
MOOLOO

Cathedral Street

St John Young Crescent

Hyde Park

College Street

Elizabeth Street

Phillip
Park

Cook
Park

(10)

Bourke Street

Forbes Street

KING'S
CROSS

Darlinghurst Road

(19)

Roslyn St

Ward Road

(20)

RUSHCUTTERS
BAY

Rushcutters
Bay Park

Park Street

William Street

Bayswater Road

King's Cross Road

Craig End Street

McLachlan Avenue

Barncleuth Ave

Kellett Street

Hyde Park

Elizabeth Street

College Street

Liverpool Street

Yurong Lane

Stanley Street

Riley Street

Crown Street

Palmer Street

Forbes Street

Bourke Street

Claxton Place

Farrell Avenue

West Womerah Avenue

Surry Street

Barcom Avenue

(21)

(25)

(27)

(22)

(23)

(26)

Victoria Street

(24)

Liverpool St

Boundary Street

Yurong Street

Liverpool Street

Burton Street

(29)

(28)

Oxford Street

Burton Street

DARLINGHURST

Darlinghurst Road

Victoria Street

Oxford Street

Barcom Avenue

Boundary Street

SURRY HILLS

PADDINGTON

Approximate scale

1/2 kilometre

1/4 mile

Considered at best, bohemian and decadent, at worst, dangerous and depraved, the suburbs immediately east of the CBD – Woolloomooloo, Potts Point and Darlinghurst – have recently been transformed into some of the most happening enclaves of Sydney. They are areas where backpackers rub shoulders with junkies, transvestite prostitutes, sailors, writers and young professionals wanting an apartment with that all important harbour view.

With its drop outs, homeless people and other shady characters there's still a jangling hard-edged reality to Woolloomooloo, Sydney's oldest suburb. Named by the Womerah people who lived here before colonization, it is largely covered by a public housing estate that was built in the 1970s, its Aboriginal roots evidenced by a few colourful murals. Its gentrification was kickstarted at the end of the 1990s by the redevelopment of the historic 400-metre-long Cowper Wharf into apartments, a private marina, a string of stylish waterside restaurants and the W hotel with the award-winning Water Bar (p. 153). Nearby is the recently renovated Tilbury Hotel (p. 155), the chic antique business The House of Green (p. 47) and several galleries, including Artspace opposite the wharf and the Soho Gallery near the suburb's coffee house of choice Toby's Estate (p. 47).

Climb the steep steps from the bay to emerge in the leafy and desirable residential streets of Potts Point. Several old hotels around here and towards Elizabeth Bay have been gutted and are being made into designer apartments. This has stoked a mini-boom of interior-design shops along Macleay Street, the suburb's main thoroughfare, while around Challis Avenue (p. 48) there is a cluster of casual restaurants and cafés catering to the style set. Where Potts Point merges with the sex-and-drugs strip of King's Cross the infamous 24-hour pub Bourbon & Beefsteak has undergone a major nip and tuck to become just simply The Bourbon, a svelte, no-fights-here-mate venue for the cocktail crowd.

South of the mammoth Coca-Cola sign over traffic clogged William Street is Darlinghurst, the hippest of this trio of suburbs. Speared by the sculptural Horizon apartment building looming over a low-rise warren of Victorian terraces, 'Darlo' is home to movie auteur Baz Luhrmann, actor Hugo Weaving, Tropfest, the biggest short movie festival in the world, and many a struggling artist, several of whom studied at the art college based in the handsome sandstone former jail on Burton Street. It also has more than its fair share of latte-serving cafés, prime locations to practise urban trend spotting.

Public ground since 1888, the Domain stretches from St Mary's Cathedral in the south to the tip of Mrs Macquarie's Point, created when in 1816 the governor's wife, Elizabeth Macquarie, decided she'd like a nice view of the harbour. She had convicts build a road to the end of the promontory to the east of Farm Cove and cut a seat in the sandstone. Millions of people have followed in her footsteps, especially for wedding photos and the perfect perch to view Sydney's spectacular harbour fireworks displays on New Year's Eve. On the Farm Cove side a section is fenced off each summer for the open air cinema. On the Woolloomooloo Bay side is the Andrew (Boy) Charlton Pool, a 50-metre-long outdoor seawater pool given a makeover in 2002, named after one of Sydney's Olympic swimmers. The heart of the Domain is the large common opposite the Art Gallery of New South Wales, where all Sydney gathers on Saturday nights in January for massive community picnics with free performances of jazz, classical music and opera.

There haven't been wheels on Harry's Cafe for several decades – this Woolloomooloo dining institution doesn't need to make the rounds of the bay to find customers for its crisp, fresh pies anymore. They line up for a 'tiger' – a chunky beef pie topped with a mound of mashed potato, mushy peas and gravy. It's a combination named in honour of Harry 'Tiger' Edwards, the ex-digger (soldier) who started selling pies from a van in 1945. The business was taken over by Michael Hannah in 1988, and it's his Hannah's pies that are now sold from this concrete bound metal shack. Photos of Rolf Harris, Kylie Minogue, Olivia Newton John, Sir Elton John and a host of local luminaries are framed on the side of the shack. Even Colonel Sanders is snapped getting his chops around a pie. Drop by late at night for the quintessential Sydney post-pub experience.

Established in 1874 the Art Gallery of New South Wales houses some of the finest art in Australia with works by major Australian artists including Tom Roberts, Arthur Streeton, Margaret Preston, Sydney Nolan, Grace Cossington Smith and Brett Whiteley. It's particularly notable for its wonderful collection of indigenous art in the Yiribana Gallery; look out for the Pukumani grave posts and *Fruit Bats* by Lin Onus – cross-hatch painted bats hanging off an iconic Hill Hoist laundry dryer. Also take time to explore the gallery's collection of statues dotted around the building, including a Henry Moore and Brett Whiteley's enigmatic giant matchsticks.

Its fabulous Asian art collection is now displayed in a two level gallery, designed by Phillip Johnson, opened in October 2003. This latest architectural addition to the gallery has a flexible, light-flooded interior affording tantalizing glimpses of the harbour, an additional bonus as you peruse the exhibits. One of the gallery's most popular exhibitions is the annual Archibald Prize competition for portraiture. Named after Jules Francois Archibald, who bequeathed the prize money in 1919, the competition winners draw large crowds every March to May.

Perhaps it's the patronage of the English backpacker crowd from King's Cross that gives the Old Fitzroy Hotel a somewhat Anglo feel. But people also come here for the steaming bowls of laksa and stir fries as much as the grog. There's a verandah at the back and a cosy upstairs bar, but what really sets the 'Fitz' apart is the studio theatre hosting an exciting and varied range of fringe productions. Plays by David Hare and Kenneth Lonergan have been put on here as well as ones by local talents. Their combined beer, laksa and theatre tickets constitute, perhaps, Sydney's best value night of entertainment.

9 Soho & Yu
171 Victoria Street

Long time Potts Point residents lament the passing of the Art-Déco Soho Bar. While the ritzy exterior is intact, little remains of the original 1930s interior beyond the pale green and cream tiles lining the hallway and stairs to the first floor cocktail lounge. Check out the glittery Gold Room, the breezy balcony and the purple baize pool tables. Downstairs, the contemporary incarnation of the Soho, combined with hip dance club Yu, makes for a fun night out, not least because of its excellent cocktail list. At least 12 new cocktails are devised each season, although some, such as the mixed berry caipiroska or the vodka, nashi pear and lychee flavoured Castaway, remain firm fixtures.

ROASTING DAILY
10 Toby's Estate
129 Cathedral Street

Toby Smith worked on coffee plantations in Brazil before returning to Sydney to open this roasting house and espresso bar. The huge Toper roaster at the back pumps out heady aromas as it churns 30 kilograms of beans at a time from Toby's selection of 40 single-origin coffees – their bold Woolloomooloo blend combines beans from India, Sumartra, Tanzania and Papua New Guinea. Sample a cup prepared by their expert baristas – they train coffee makers and you can take a class to learn how to get the best from your home espresso machine. Eighteen types of tea are available, including four house blends, as well as tasty focaccia sandwiches, rice paper and nori rolls and delicious cakes. While in the area, drop by the Soho Gallery at the corner of Cathedral and Crown Streets – there's usually an interesting exhibition on. Opposite the East Sydney Hotel, dating from 1856, is a charming throwback to the time when Sydney pubs were not just excuses for gambling at the pokies; it's one of the few hotel's without slot machines.

TIME FOR DESIGN
11 Macleay on Manning
85 Macleay Street

Jill and Rod Ordish have assembled a bumper crop of interior goodies at their designer homewares store. Besides the stripey Missoni towels, perspex Philippe Starck stools and David Edmunds ceramics are unusual pieces such as the noodle chair – a woven water-hyacinth recliner – and large cow fur cushions. There's a great range of baby wear, including cute sheepskin boots and towelling teddy bears;

the child in everyone will want the giant pencils and erasers. And for the style guru with an international schedule, there's a set of five clocks on coloured glass tiles telling you the time from London to Tokyo.

NEOCLASSICAL VILLA
12 Royal Australian Institute of Architects
Tusculum, 3 Manning Street

In 1984 the Royal Institute of Architects came to the rescue of Tusculum, a grand villa dating from the 1830s, designed by John Verge for the Scottish colonial merchant A. B. Spark. It's a handsome building with a two-storey Ionic colonnade thrown into relief by the modern building the Institute commissioned to sit beside it. Running in a convex curve of concrete at the rear of the site, the new wing houses the excellent architecture bookshop Architext, offices of the institute and an auditorium.

TWENTIETH-CENTURY CLASSICS
13 Tyrone Dearing
12 Macleay Street

Tyrone Dearing's elegant collection is displayed in this small showroom beside the entrance to the grand Macleay Regis apartments. You can imagine his classic 20th-century pieces going very well in these Déco-era homes. His range starts with Secessionist pieces from Vienna and focuses on the best of European design up until the late 1950s. Works by Adnet, Prou, Borsani and Barovier rub shoulders with key Australian designers of the period. Much in demand for his interior-design services, Dearing also designs and manufactures his own range of furniture and accessories, which he plans to feature more prominently in the gallery in the future.

BREAK THE RULES
14 The House of Green
84–85 Nicholson Street

Follow your instincts rather than design rules at the wonderfully quirky The House of Green antiques and art shop. Owner Alison Green recently moved her collection of mainly French and Italian decorative furnishings here from Annandale, where she set up shop in 1999. She has a great eye for whimsical detail and eccentric, indulgent pieces that can be mixed and matched to create your own slice of Australian bohemia. You'll find 1930s Toleware lamps from Argentina beside the contemporary outback paintings of John Murray, or Lionel Lindsay woodblock prints next to 1960s leather loungers.

A cluster of appealing lunch spots has formed at the Macleay Street end of Challis Avenue. Next door to Lotus, Fratelli Paradiso is run by the Paradiso brothers from Melbourne. They've brought to Sydney a big helping of Bleak City's style in modern Italian cooking. Inspect the blackboard opposite the Andy Warholesque wallpaper of spaghetti munching lips for the daily specials. They also run the delicious pasticceriea next door. Opposite is La Buvette with a delightful menu of fresh salads, gourmet pies and sweet cakes. Hot competition on the dessert front comes from newly opened Yellow Bistro & Food Store around the corner, occupying 1970s arts-scene landmark The Yellow House. It's run by George Sinclair and Lorraine Godsmark who made their name in Sydney by creating fabulous desserts at their last business, Six Seven Ate. Fortified with good food, give your wallet a workout at Arida, a well-edited interior design shop on the corner of Challis Avenue. It stocks a super stylish selection of items ranging from Moroccan silk and suede slippers to antique Japanese sake flasks.

Elizabeth Bay House's outstanding interior, with its cantilevered staircase sweeping down from an oval dome, is rightly considered one of the finest examples of its kind in Australia. Designed by John Verge and completed in 1839, the house was built for Colonial Secretary Alexander Macleay and has been furnished by the Historic Houses Trust of New South Wales, its current custodians, to reflect his occupancy during the mid-19th century. In front a small, neat patch of park affords a splendid view across yacht-dotted Elizabeth Bay.

If you're looking for a late night party with characters on every barstool, this smoky den is the place to come. The recent upgrading of the Bourbon & Beefsteak pub has left Baron's as practically the sole trustee of the true bohemian spirit of the Cross. With its nicotine-stained walls, musty carpet, clubby leather armchairs, backgammon tables and dimly lit bar it seems as if it has been here since the dawn of time but, in fact, the legend began in 1979. Downstairs used to be a French restaurant; it's now Thai, but that's about all that's changed in a place that still guarantees a warm welcome and a devilishly strong cocktail to anyone who rocks up past the witching hour.

Running behind the giant Coca-Cola sign that pinpoints King's Cross, Bayswater Road is where you'll find long-running Bayswater Brasserie, a classic world of starched tablecloths, bentwood chairs and hearty, good value brasserie–style cuisine. It's all very relaxed, and the bar at the back has a tree-shaded courtyard where you can smoke. Over the road and upstairs is Hugo's Lounge, the inner city sibling of Bondi's Hugo's (p. 82). The beautiful people who quaff cocktails on the balcony or groove along to lounge music while they pick at the overwrought mod-Oz dishes seem to think they've found the right place. It can get precious, but slip into the right designer outfit, adopt an attitude and you might just fit in.

OYSTERS -
ROCKS - CAMDEN HAVEN, HASTINGS RIVER,
BELLINGER RIVER, MACLEAY RIVER 2.90

OLIVE BREAD 4.50
GRILLED TASMANIAN HALF SHELL SCALLOPS w
SORREL + TOMATO BUTTER 21.00

JEWFISH FILLET w SPRING VEGETABLES w ARUGA
29.50

ROASTED PORK CUTLET w POTATO RÖSTI,
WATERCRESS SOUP, APPLE + CALVADOS
SAUCE 28.00

* CHOCOLATE TORTE w BAILEYS ICE CREAM 12.50

25 Victoria Street

- Tropicanna Caffe, no. 227
- Bar Coluzzi, no, 322
- Latteria, no. 320
- Peel, no. 274
- de Cjuba, nos 314–18
- Provedore Pelagio, no. 235
- Infinity Sourdough Bakery, no, 225
- Will & Toby's, nos 292–94, level 1

Cafés abound at the southern end of Victoria Street. The Tropicanna Caffe, famed for its hearty salads in metal bowls, is where Sydney's favourite short-film festival gets its name from. A lot of business also seems to be conducted over lattes or long blacks by the crowds perched on milk crates and tree stumps in front of Bar Coluzzi, a Victoria Street institution. Next door Latteria offers a similar menu of strong coffees and snacks for the exec. on the run.

If you're in no hurry you may want to cruise the shops, including Peel for clubbing fashions and the more dressy de Cjuba. Or you could go grocery shopping at Provedore Pelagio, the street's most tempting deli, then drop by the Infinity Sourdough Bakery. Run by Phillip Searle, whose Vulcans restaurant in Blackheath is legendary, they bake a full range of delicious sourdough breads. For alcoholic drinks – apart from The Victoria Room – there's Will & Toby's intimate cocktail bar.

26 Darlinghurst Road

- Ken Neale, no. 138
- Darlo Bar, no. 306
- Ecabar, no. 128
- Fishface, no. 132

The reason many people come to Darlinghurst Road is to explore the latest offerings at Ken Neale's shop. His collection of classic 20th-century furniture, mainly from the 1950s onwards, includes a range of formica-topped tables unparalleled in Sydney. He also carries lights, ceramics, glass and rugs from the 1960s and 1970s. The retro furniture in the Darlo Bar at the Royal Sovereign Hotel could all have come from Ken's. This is one of the area's most convivial bars, famous for its pool table presided over by Reggie, the Cool Hand Luke of Darlinghurst. Equally hip with the in-crowd and bikers is the wedge-shaped Ecabar; they always have interesting art on the orange walls and great coffee and snacks. Fishface is back in action after a makeover that has seen the addition of a sushi bar and some top class fish'n'chips served in a cone.

27 Bruno Dutot
120A Darlinghurst Road

Oucha has had her elegant back turned on the world since 1989 when French artist Bruno Dutot painted her at various public locations around the city. The most famous spot is on the corner of Darling Point Road and New South Head Road in Edgecliff. Since 2001 Dutot has been selling his paintings of this enigmatic beauty with the tapering arms and little black cat from a makeshift gallery on one side of a carwash station opposite Salt restaurant (p. 135). He likes to use alternative canvases for his art, including hessian, cardboard, old signs and cupboard draws. Sydney has taken Oucha to their hearts, much like the iconic *Eternity* scribbled by Arthur Stace decades before, making her a modern symbol of the city.

28 Chicane

156

29 Palmer Street

- Red Leather, no. 298
- TAP Gallery, no. 278, level 1
- House of Shanghai, no. 171
- Pizza Mario, no. 248

The Burley Katon Halliday designed Republic 2 complex of apartments on Palmer Street has brought an injection of urban professional life to an area that once was the heart of nefarious East Sydney. Not that those enjoying alternative lifestyles have fled the area altogether. Keeping the flag flying for diversity is Red Leather run by Scott Bird. Starting with belts, cuffs and wallets, and moving all the way up to slings and leather covered bones (they're not for real dogs), Bird's leatherwork and that of Demon Leather, which he also stocks, is of the finest quality and is aimed at a younger, fashion-conscious crowd. TAP Gallery is a space for emerging artists with a café similar to your mad Aunt Mildred's living room and a small theatre studio at the back. Ani creates exotic Asian bead jewelry and stocks other Chinese objet d'art at her House of Shanghai boutique. Back at the Republic Square with its lumpy metal sculpture and patchwork of sandstone blocks, Pizza Mario sticks to a strict code of pizza making: no variation of ingredients and no half and half. No one's complaining since the huge thin-crust pizzas are so good.

Surry Hills
Waterloo

HAYMARKET

DARLINGHURST

PADDINGTON

SURRY HILLS

REDFERN

MOORE PARK

WATERLOO

Approximate scale

1/2 kilometre

1/4 mile

Sydney is the gay and lesbian capital of Australia, and nowhere is this more apparent than in Surry Hills and neighbouring Darlinghurst. Delineating these two suburbs is Oxford Street, which, from its origin at the southeast corner of Hyde Park to the junction with South Dowling Street, is the gay community's parade ground. Every March hundreds of thousands of people gather here to cheer on the fabulous Gay and Lesbian Mardi Gras parade, always preceded by the revving phalanx of Dykes on Bikes. For an insight into the history and characters of the area peek into the information pods sprouting from Taylor Square. After what seemed an eternity of construction, this patch of multicoloured paving and spurting fountains at the junction of Oxford, Bourke and Flinders Streets was unveiled in November 2003. Next in line for a makeover is Oxford Street itself with plans for wider pavements, better street furniture, more trees and consistent signage and shop fronts.

While breathing much joi de vivre into the undulating district, the gay community is not Surry Hills' only inhabitants. Sydney's rag trade is clustered around Forveaux Street – Rupert Murdoch's newspapers *The Australian* and *The Daily Telegraph* are produced here – and the area has a strong reputation for interior-design and furniture stores. The huddled Victorian terraces have attracted a spill over of house hunters from Paddington where prices have already escalated. Surry Hills is going the same way, while retaining a grittier, less prettified edge. The elements that attracted artists such as Brett Whiteley here are still present – check out his old studio (p. 61) on a diversion from Crown Street, along which you'll find Sydney's most outstanding portfolio of restaurants and some highly individual boutiques.

At the southern foot of Crown Street is Cleveland Street, which marks the border of Surry Hills with Redfern, home to Sydney's remaining Aboriginal community and one of the inner city's most deprived areas. The worst precincts are by Redfern railway station, but on the whole Redfern, like Surry Hills, is on the up, with its run-down real estate providing tempting bargains for property developers and speculators. In particular, Waterloo, the suburb on the east side of Redfern, largely occupied by light industry and warehouses, is becoming one of the hot places to live and shop. A complex of chic apartments and amenities, including the new Object Store gallery, will open in 2004 on the old St Margaret's Hospital site on Bourke Street, and the heritage-listed Railway Institute building on Chalmers Street is being transformed into the Pacific Club, an exclusive and arty private club along the lines of London's Groucho Club.

1 Oxford Street West

- Zink & Sons, no. 56
- Sax Fetish, no. 110A
- The Bookshop Darlinghurst, no. 207
- The Columbian, nos 117–23
- The Oxford, no. 134

With its assortment of tawdry sex and discount shops, must-have-a-new-clubbing-outfit stores and cafés and bars with big open windows and outdoor seating for maximum cruising opportunities, you may wonder what is all the fuss about Oxford Street. There are some interesting shops – drop by the traditional tailors Zink & Sons with its gorgeous Art-Déco façade, Sax Fetish for the very latest in leather, latex and lurex gear or The Bookshop to see what the community is reading about – but bear in mind the shopping opportunities improve exponentially at the Paddington end of the street (p. 66). It's really after dark that this section comes into its own. The Columbian, the pumping two-level bar in an old bank on the corner of Crown and Oxford Streets, is the place to meet and greet. Upstairs, the mood gets more chilled with leather sofas to lounge in and later a DJ spins tracks that are sure to have you dancing before the night is over. The Oxford has a prime position overlooking Taylor Square and its cocktail bars – Gilligans and Gingers on levels one and two respectively – are the place for a civilized drink, while the ground floor is more hectic and crowded.

The City of Sydney has grand plans to upgrade this part of Oxford Street but, following on from the massive yawn that greeted the unveiling of the long-awaited revamp of Taylor Square, no one is holding their breath for anything too fabulous.

NOUVELLE JAPANESE
2 Uchi Lounge
15 Brisbane Street

Tucked down a narrow lane off Oxford Street is Uchi Lounge, a hip, modern Japanese restaurant popular with the stylish set. In the main dining area upstairs, divided by gauze screens and enhanced by moody lighting, indulge in a refreshingly different menu of Japanese-influenced delights. Their salty-sweet grilled aubergine with miso and parmesan is a nod to Japan's *mukokuseki* (no-nationality) style of cuisine found at the country's most innovative restaurants and bars. The Tampopo sushi switches the usual oblongs of vinegared rice and fish into pretty balls. Heavy jade-coloured crockery and high-quality wooden chopsticks add to the experience. There's

a no booking policy, but you can wait for a table in the bar downstairs and try one of the sake-based cocktails. They also serve a mean Bloody Mary spiced with chili, and intriguing snacks such as lemon infused soya beans.

NEW ASIAN GROOVE
3 Longrain

SNARE A MILLIONAIRE
4 Wheels & Doll Baby

168

STUCK IN THE MIDDLE WITH YOU
5 Middle Bar

155

MATERIAL WORLD
6 Nick Brown
397 Bourke Street

Sydney-based designers making interesting clothes for men are few and far between, but Nick Brown, an alumnus of Paddington Markets, comes to the rescue. Brown has been in his tiny shop and cutting room just off Taylor Square for a decade, starting the business with former partner Louise Tuckwell. Although their joint label is still used, it's just Brown working on the clothes now; Tuckwell's contribution is left to the colourful geometric paintings on the walls. Brown's clothes are set apart by his choice of fabrics, which include broderie anglaise, chenille, fine cotton voile and quilted textiles. As well as off the peg clothes, Brown can tailor to individual specifications. He imports a range of colourful hand-knitted beanies from India, and you can accessorize with the bead jewelry of Michelle Edinger.

ROCKSTAR PLAYGROUND
7 Moog Hotel

FUEL-INJECTED FOOD
8 MG Garage

136

9 Crown Street

- Marque, no. 355
- Café Mint, no. 579
- Clock Hotel, no. 470
- Chee Soon & Fitzgerald, no. 387
- Planet Furniture, no. 419
- Mrs Red & Sons, no. 427
- Hanksta, no. 346
- Chetcuti Boutique – Coco Monkey Interiors, no. 340

Crown Street, from its junction with Oxford Street to its southern terminus at Cleveland Street, is so happening that you could easily spend a whole day browsing in its fashion boutiques and interior-design stores in between dining at some of the most celebrated restaurants in Sydney. French cooking of the finest quality is provided by Mark Best at Marque; his beetroot tart made with the crispiest pastry is legendary. At the Cleveland Street end Café Mint is a stylishly designed box with a Turkish slant to its offerings, including sweet couscous for breakfast and lamb shanks braised with pomegranate. The Clock Hotel is a good example of a how to make an old pub a modern classic – cool, open design downstairs, a sophisticated but casual restaurant with balcony seating upstairs. Interior designers flock to Chee Soon & Fitzgerald for their heavenly collection of fabrics and wallpapers from Thailand and Finland, as well as the ceramics and the Wovo Torso lamps and lightshades by Australia's Marc Pascal. The sleek, sturdy furniture of Ross Longmuir at Planet Furniture is made from sustainable timbers – his store also specializes in handcrafted textiles and ceramics: Ruth Macmillan's work is particularly notable. Mrs Red & Sons stocks highly desirable Asian and Asian-influenced homewares and gifts – all beautifully gift wrapped. Wrapping yourself up nicely is easily achieved at the funky duo of boutiques Hanksta and Chetcuti Boutique – Coco Monkey Interiors: both offer quirky clothes and pop-art ephemera for the body and home.

CONTEMPORARY CHINESE
10 Billy Kwong
335 Crown Street, shop 3

Proving what a democratic dining scene Sydney has, along comes another restaurant with a no booking policy, but the queues are long at this phenomenally popular modern Chinese eatery. Even before Kylie Kwong produced a best-selling cookbook and prime-time TV show on the ABC, there were crowds at her cramped, frenetic restaurant – a modern take on the Shanghai teahouse. The word was

out that this graduate of Neil Perry's Rockpool (p. 130) was the girl to watch. Her signature dish is crispy skin duck with fresh blood-orange sauce, but she also does great things with fish. The only quibble is that the black varnished wooden stools are pretty uncomfortable, but maybe that's a conscious decision to get those adoring customers in and out as quickly as possible.

MODERN LIVING
11 Koskela Design
91 Campbell Street, level 1

Surry Hills Central is a collective of seven furniture and homeware showrooms specializing in local and imported contemporary design, all clustered in the garment district around Commonwealth Street. One of the most interesting is Koskela Design, a showroom for the modern, uncomplicated furniture of Russel Koskela. Together with his partner, Sasha Tichkosky, Koskela started the interior-design company in 2000; his sled base table was chosen to be part of Australia's Hybrid Objects exhibition at the Tokyo Designers Block of 2002, and in 2004 his work was seen at the Modern White Exhibition in Berlin. His 'kids clubs' range of playful and stylish mini furniture will appeal to design-conscious mums and dads, as will the kangaroo 'rocking horse' toys from Denmark, contemporary ceramics and designer teatowels stocked in this first floor New York loft like space.

THE ART OF JEWELRY
12 Gallery Onefivesix
156 Commonwealth Street

Run by jewelry designers Michael Pell and John Ewan, Gallery Onefivesix showcases contemporary Australian jewelry in a range of metals, from traditional gold and silver to the more unusual palladium and titanium. Around 60 jewelry and objet d'art designers from around the country are represented in the six-to-eight exhibitions each year at this industrial space. You'll find avant-garde pieces that embrace a freer, more organic style and approach to metalwork.

SOFT TO TOUCH
13 Customweave Carpets & Rugs
171

ONE STOP STYLE
14 Orson & Blake
174

15 Bécasse
48 Albion Street

Justin North is a young Sydney chef whose fine modern French cooking keeps on scoring rave reviews. His wife and business partner, Georgina Lawrence-Slater, keeps the front of house moving so smoothly that all the attention is focused on the delicious morsels on the plate. North's daily changing menu reflects the season's best produce and his skill at the stoves: it could be pan-fried Hiramasa kingfish with cauliflower puree and horseradish chantilly or caramelized calves' sweetbreads. The rustic desserts get top marks too; the strawberry and rhubarb *tarte fine* is a particularly good example of North's rich Gallic craft.

LIFE IS BRIEF...
16 Brett Whiteley Studio
2 Raper Street

'...but my god Thursday afternoon seems incredibly long!' The grafitti scrawled on maverick Australian artist Brett Whiteley's studio wall alongside other doodles – both philosophical and silly – seems to sum him up. Life for Whiteley, one of the most talented and strikingly original Australian artists to emerge in the early 1960s, was not so brief as he may have assumed. A heroin addict since the 1970s, he struggled with his demons and transferred some of that angst and fevered imagination to his artworks before finally succumbing in 1992, aged 53. The epic *Alchemy* that spans two walls of his last working studio dazzles and disturbs with its whacked out vision of the beauty and horror of life. Although some parts of the studio have been left as they were when Whiteley died, it is not a slavish memorial. The exhibitions, drawn from the collection of the Art Gallery of New South Wales and the artist's estate, change regularly, and many of Whiteley's curious collections of objects – his badges, sunglasses, hats, even his records and CDs – have been arranged like mini artworks. The studio is only open at weekends.

THE COMPANY YOU KEEP
17 Belvoir Street Theatre
25 Belvoir Street

Neil Armfield's Company B, whose home is the Belvoir Street Theatre, is one of the most acclaimed theatre troupes in Australia: Geoffrey Rush, Cate Blanchett and Richard Roxburgh are just some of the top acting talent who have made their name here. The season of productions leaps around from revisited classics such as *What the Butler Saw*, to big gun imports and dazzling home grown plays like *Cloudstreet*, which received ovations all over the world. There are two stages – the Upstairs Theatre seating 350 and the intimate 80-seater Downstairs space hosting fringe companies. The building, once a tomato-sauce factory, gained prominence in the 1970s as the Nimrod Theatre. Martin Sharp's posters for Nimrod productions are graphic-design classics. In 1984 the building was saved from demolition by a syndicate of over 600 arts and media professionals who clubbed together to buy the theatre.

ORIENTAL TEASHOP
18 Zensation
656 Bourke Street

Raymond Leung's successful interior-design, marketing and promotion company is responsible for, among other things, the modern Asian interior of East Ocean in Chinatown, (p. 37). He worked with Ric Birch on the fabulous harbour pageant that heralded the 2000 Olympics. A mini version of the painted fabric fish lanterns that Leung designed for that event, which caused a sensation at the time, can be bought at his interior-design shop Zensation. It stocks an eclectic mix of feng shui–style water features, lacquerware, antique bird cages and Shanghai 1940s–style print T-shirts. At the rear Leung indulges passions for tea – there are 50 different types from China and Japan, all prepared in the traditional way.

THE NEW GREEK
19 Café Zoe
688 Bourke Street

Café Zoe's heritage-green paint scheme teamed with a chocolate leather banquet and stained-wood chairs will not win any awards for originality. But the addition of a black-and-white Florence Broadhurst print panel and a sculpted wooden wall by the open kitchen suggest a creative flair fulfiled by the elegant style of the food. Head chef John Stavropolous brings his Greek background to bear in a short but sweet menu that captures the mood of the season. A hearty lentil, lemon and silverbeet soup might look sludgy but it tastes delicious, likewise the Ismir meatballs with stuffed green olives in a rich tomato sauce. Whether you drop by for a coffee and cake or a relaxing meal at night, the service is always prompt and friendly.

ARTS CENTRAL
20 Danks Street Depot
146

Paddington
Woollahra
Double Bay
Rose Bay

PORT
JACKSON

Shark
Island

Clark
Island

POTTS
POINT

ELIZABETH
BAY

Elizabeth
Bay

Elizabeth
Point

Macleay
Point

Rushcutters
Bay

RUSHCUTTERS
BAY

Rushcutters
Bay
Park

McKell
Park

Darling
Point

DARLING
POINT

Point
Piper

Felix
Bay

Woollahra
Point

POINT
PIPER

Blackburn
Cove

Rose
Bay
Park

Rose
Bay

27

29

Double
Bay

New South Head Road

Victoria Road

Steyne
Park

William Street

23 **28**
26
24

Greenoaks Ave

Ocean Avenue

21
22

Cooper Street

Holt Street

25

DOUBLE
BAY

Ginahgulla Road

Victoria Road

Drumalbyn Road

O'Sullivan Road

Powell Road

Plumer Road

New South Head Road

EDGECLIFF

Kiaora Lane

Kiaora Road

Bellevue Road

Manning Road

Edgecliffe Road

Victoria Street

1

West Wandella Avenue

Barcom Avenue

Surrey Street

McLachlan Avenue

Neild Avenue

New Beach Road

Mona Road

Darling Point Road

Albert Street

Glenmore Road

PADDINGTON

Gurner Street

5

Cascade Street

Trumper
Park

Trelawney Street

WOOLLAHRA

Ocean Street

Victoria Street

Boundary Street

Macdonald

Glenmore Road

Gipps Street

4

2

Napier Street

Albion Avenue

3

Hargrave Street

Underwood Street

9
10
7 **8**

Moore Park Road

14 **6**

Renny Street

Jersey Road

20
12 **16** **18** **19**
13 **17**

Moncur St

15

Queen Street

Wellington St

Fiveash Street

Wallis Street

Edgecliff Road

Syd Einfeld Drive

BELLEVUE
HILL

Cooper
Park

View Street

Bathurst
St

Fletcher Street

Edgecliffe Road

Old South Head Road

Birriga

Sydney
Football
Stadium

Sydney
Cricket
Ground

Fox
Studios
Australia

Moore
Park

Driver Avenue

Lang Road

Cook Road

Oxford Street

Parkes Drive

Carrington Drive

York Road

BONDI
JUNCTION

BONDI

Approximate scale

1 kilometre

1/2 mile

Anzac Parade

Lang Road

Robertson Road

Dickens Drive

Grand Drive

Parkes Drive

11

CENTENNIAL
PARK

QUEENS
PARK

MOORE
PARK

Alison Road

Darley Road

Queens
Park

WAVERLEY

Serious shoppers should head to Paddington, Woollahra and Double Bay, Sydney's most scenic trio of suburbs. Paddington's delightful cottages and pastel painted terraces decorated with iron balconies and railings were the slum dwellings of the city's working classes, but are now the domain of the cashed-up chattering classes and, despite the lack of space, rising damp and cockroaches that are part and parcel of terrace living, the best of these homes sell for over $1 million.

Any disposable income is easily soaked up by Paddo's bumper bundle of sophisticated boutiques and delectable restaurants and cafés. Most are found cheek by jowl along Oxford Street – everything from top international brands Ben Sherman and French Connection to local success stories such as Dinosaur Designs and Zimmermann, who got their start at Saturday's unmissable Paddington Market (p. 69), prime hunting ground for the next hit fashion. For a more intimate taste of the suburb's charming style explore north of Oxford Street opposite the sandstone wall of Victoria Barracks: wind your way past the galleries of Glenmore Road to the gourmet nexus of Five Ways (p. 66), and then boutique-packed William Street (p. 68). South of Oxford Street are the Sydney Football Stadium and Sydney Cricket Ground, attracting massive crowds to sporting events and pop concerts, and Fox Studios where *Moulin Rouge*, the *Matrix* trilogy and most recent *Star Wars* movies were filmed. The old Sydney showground site contains a couple of multiplex cinemas, the populist Bent Street shopping and dining strip, and a regular growers' market.

The shopping possibilities are more salubrious in Woollahra, which begins where Oxford Street meets Centennial Park. The triangle formed by Queen Street, Ocean Street and Jersey Road contains an upmarket village of pricey antique shops, galleries (including branches of Sotheby's and Christie's), boutiques and quality food retailers. The somewhat snooty atmosphere – think haughty women with immaculate hairdos, make-up and designer outfits – continues down the hill in Double Bay, Sydney's most luxurious shopping precinct. It's a compact and eclectic place; next to old-world institutions such as the Cosmopolitan café, where grannies tuck into chicken soup with matzo-ball dumplings, are trendy boutiques such as Paablo Nevada and Marcs. During the spring months of October and November the profusion of the jacaranda trees' purple blossoms dominate. These beautiful Brazilian trees were introduced to Sydney in the mid-19th century by the gardener Michael Guilfoyle, after whom one of Double Bay's streets is named. East over the hill is the broad, yacht-dotted expanse of Rose Bay where sea planes take off, and where you'll find a couple of Sydney's best waterside restaurants.

Known as Sydney's golden mile of shopping, from the junction with South Dowling Street to the gates of Centennial Park, Oxford Street offers up an embarrassment of shopping riches. You're going to need a smart bag so start at Crumpler: these tough, colourful Australian bags in a range of sizes and styles are the choice of speedy, trend-conscious couriers and photographers on the go. The Jeremy Store is the headquarters of UK artist Peter Fowler's whacky world of Monsterism, The Hazkems (Hazardous Chemical Kids) and Jeremyville. It's a twisted sort of cartoon land, but it's worth checking out the graphic art T-shirts, 3D figures and lightboxes. Some T-shirts have maps on them so you should be able to find your way home, or at least to Sweet Art, a shrine to the art of cake icing. The fabulous designs range from bunches of realistic flowers to Marge and Homer Simpson in the bath.

Start assembling a new wardrobe from the glamourous, hooker-chic clothes of Alannah Hill and Bracewell's selection of Sass & Bide's must-have jeans and high-fashion lines alongside their own collection. Guys get a fashion look in at Joe Saba's menswear store – his equally elegant womenswear can be found at 39 Bay Street in Double Bay. Marcs and Wayne Cooper both have contemporary clothing for either sex, and Clifford Gordon offers his own brand of fashion made from sensational rock-star fabrics – expect suits in striped velvet and

unsubtle patterned shirts. There has been an influx of designers from Melbourne along this stretch: Déclic sells Gilles Du Puy's fine quality cotton and linen shirts; Scanlan & Theodore's womenswear is known for its subvertive take on classic styles, combining floaty fabrics with leather tassles, lace and sequins; and Mimco produces playful bags, jewelry, belts and sunhats. And this is just the tip of the consumer iceberg! Time to rest and revive at Bistro Lulu, another in Luke Mangan and Lucy Allon's growing empire of top-class Sydney restaurants. It is a wonderfully relaxed place for a casual French meal and a glass of decent wine, and next door is the Centre for Photography, which frequently has an interesting exhibition on.

The shopping hub of Five Ways is at the intersection of four Paddington streets – Glenmore Road, Heeley Street, Broughton Street and Goodhope Street. There's a village feel to the area with the handsome, iron-lace decorated Royal Hotel, dating from 1888, acting as the local pub, and restaurants and cafés crowding around the other corners. Gusto, with its street tables and tempting range of dishes, is a good option as is the stylish new Booker's , which combines a deli, wine bar and restaurant in one attractive package – the frangipani-shaded courtyard at the back is a pleasant retreat for a long lunch. Paul & Joe, opposite, a spin-off from Double Bay's Christensen Copenhagen (p. 73), stocks the pretty floral and terribly French clothes of Sophie Albon. Continuing the French theme is La Gerbe d'Or, generally recognized as Sydney's best patisserie; it's the place for baguettes and croissants. It may be tiny, but the wine selection at Five Ways Cellars is one of the best in the eastern suburbs; the assistants are knowledgable about the best Australian wines available.

The terraces of William Street hold many shopping delights, starting from the Oxford Street end with Just William Chocolates, one of Sydney's longest-running confectioners. Among their tempting range of handmade chocolates are ones shaped as native Australian fauna, including echidnas and platypuses. G&L offer handmade shoes for men and women in intriguingly different designs. Sylvia Chan is one of the elder stateswomen of William Street; she's particularly well known for her hand-painted couture gowns and non-traditional wedding dresses, but her collection also covers casual and swimwear, all made with luxurious and exotic fabrics. Breaking from the more formal frocks and gowns of neighbouring stores is The Nudie House with their favourite Australian and Scandinavian T-shirts, jeans and underwear. Ex-model Belinda Semper's collection of eponymous Belinda boutiques has its chic headquarters at number 39 with a choice selection of established and up-and-coming European fashion labels. On the corner of William and Underwood Streets, the stately London Tavern, dating from 1875, is the suburb's oldest pub. Leona Edmiston, ex-business partner of Peter Morrissey, has a boutique selling well-made feminine frocks in silks and cotton prints nearby.

11 Centennial Park

Bounded by Oxford Street, York, Darley, Alison and Robertson Roads

Dedicated 'to the enjoyment of the people of New South Wales forever' on the centenary of the colony's foundation in 1888, Centennial Park is Sydney's largest public recreation ground. If you include adjacent Moore Park and Queens Park there are over 385 hectares of greenery. This reclaimed swampland, where over 100,000 people gathered on 1 January 1901 to witness the birth of the Commonwealth of Australia, is now a popular place for cyclists, horse riders, in-line skaters and people wanting to relax. In-line skates can be hired from Centennial Park Cycles, 50 Clovelly Road, closest to the Govett Street gate in Randwick, and for horse-riding contact the Centennial Parkland Equestrian Centre on the corner of Fox Studios beside the Robertson Road gates. Every summer the outdoor Moonlight Cinema sets up near the Woollahra gate.

INNOVATION & TRADITION

12 Claude's

138

MUST HAVE SWIMWEAR

13 Zimmerman

163

FASHION CRUCIBLE

14 Paddington Markets

395 Oxford Street

Many famous Australian brands – Lonely Planet, Dinosaur Designs, Zimmermann – started at Paddington Markets, held every Saturday in the grounds of the Paddington United Church since 1973. There are 250 stalls offering everything from fresh flowers and homemade jams to backrubs and pet accessories. There's also a tempting range of food-and-drink stalls and a play area for kids. The original homewares, fashion and jewelry stalls are the ones to focus on. Paulineke Polkamps's vividly coloured pottery can usually be found on the Oxford Street side. Look out for Rhynie Cawood's clothes and artworks made from her floral and abstract prints on cotton and silk – she's not a regular yet so she moves around the market. Zephyr make funky T-shirts using vintage ties for one shoulder strap, as well as leather cuffs that have already been spotted by the local fashion mags.

Queen Street is one of the most celebrity-studded streets in Sydney. The poet Banjo Patterson (of *Waltzing Matilda* fame) lived here as did opera singer Dame Joan Sutherland, and ex-Prime Minister Paul Keating and the reigning superstar of Australian talk radio, John Laws, currently have residences here. Since the 1950s the elegant Victorian terraces have also housed Sydney's finest range of antique shops and galleries. Take your pick from religious Himalayan art and erotic shunga prints from Japan at Beowulf Galleries or Australian paintings, prints, sculptures and ceramics at Rex Irwin. Lisa Ho is another designer who used the Paddington Market as a springboard to international acclaim: her frocks are now worn by movie stars at red-carpet events. Höglund Art Glass Gallery exhibits beautiful vividly coloured handblown glass by Swedish–born, New Zealand–based master glassblower Ola Höglund and his wife, Marie Simberg-Höglund, using the complex Sommerso and Graal techniques. Interesting contemporary homewares, as well as cutting edge fashion, can be found across the road at Orson & Blake (see also p. 174), and nearby the colourful Arte Flowers is a pleasant café.

The grand Italianate mansion that now houses this delightfully quirky boutique hotel was built in 1876 by Dr Frederick Quaife. When the Gervay sisters, Susanne and Elizabeth, bought it in 1992 the mansion had fallen on hard times and had become a hostel for the homeless. Even though there's still a creakiness and air of faded grandeur, the sisters have achieved wonders revitalizing the place and restoring something of its original character. Trading on the hotel's heritage value and their own artistic talents (Susanne is a writer and Elizabeth a painter) they host art exhibitions, writers' group meetings and book launches. In the convivial lobby lounge, by reservation, a full afternoon tea is served with dainty sandwiches and cakes – it's all terribly British and quite charming.

There's plenty that's fancy about jones the grocer, an upmarket shop and café for people who don't need to or care to count the pennies when they go food shopping. The greatest appeal, however, is that they make classic gourmet foods and confections – marshmallows, florentines, jams, chutneys and sauces – simply and well. Everything looks so delicious and tempting that you might stock up the larder, or at least throw together a picnic from their fresh breads, salads and cheeses to enjoy in nearby Centennial Park. Many of the products are made daily in their kitchens, and, if you can't wait to try them, there's a big communal table at which you can eat and drink.

The picturesque one-time servants' cottages of Transvaal Avenue transformed, Cinderella-like, into chic clothes and homewares stores are Double Bay at its most charming. Belinda Seper has another of her classy boutiques here, as well as a new shoe salon stocking Jimmy Choo, Sigerson Morrison, Marni and Michel Vivien. After browsing the desirable homewares of Papaya (p. 162) find a beautiful, uniquely designed rug from the colourful collection at Robyn Cosgrove Rugs. At the Cross Street end of the avenue is Paablo Nevada, where fashion designers Wayne and Betty Fong offer a sophisticated, directional look loved by the suburb's style mavens, while their PuPP label is younger, more girlie and affordable.

Reneé Coleman brought her successful homewares store, Empire, all the way from Perth to Sydney's Oxford Street, before moving to this smaller outlet in Double Bay. Touting a look that she calls 'French modern with a softer, feminine edge', Coleman is already winning over Sydney's most style-conscious suburb. The store offers design solutions for all rooms in the house, from muslin-clad soaps for the bathroom to chocolate coloured leather sofas. Melbourne company Vixen's quilts and cushions in velvet and silk are a star buy, or you could restock your kitchen with their elegantly simple white china.

With many old European immigrants on its doorstep, Double Bay is full of cafés where you can sip on strong espressos accompanied by chocolatey gateaux. Bucking this trend is Taka Tea Garden, a shrine to the health benefits of green tea. Owners Taka Pan and Helen Kwok are evangelical about the miraculous properties of this ancient beverage and, after sampling one of their 77 varieties, including the bright *gyokuro*, the dense, caffeine-rich *matcha* and the mild, rustic *genmaicha*, it's difficult not to agree with them. They also serve their special green tea cake and rice crackers. Soothing music, comfortable teal-and-cream upholstered chairs and Tasmanian oak tables add to the experience.

Chef James Constantinidis is known in Sydney for his 'Jimmy the Greek' brand of taramasalata. The tasty pink dip is on the menu at his restaurant and bar alongside aubergine topped with chargrilled scallops and lamb *exohiko* (filo pastry parcels of meat mixed with olive paste, Kefalotyri cheese and wilted spinach). With a live band at weekends it can be an unusually lively place for Double Bay, especially if the crowd is in the mood for a bit of 'Zorba'–style dancing and plate smashing. The mix of modern and traditional Greek dishes, an ice-blue luminous bar and al-fresco dining at dazzling white tables at the front, conjures up a lazy night on an idyllic Aegean island.

Marianne Christensen ran a designer boutique in Copenhagen before moving to Australia and opening this business in 1998. It quickly established its reputation for providing the finest of the current season's collections from Europe. In a chic space dominated by a glowing aquarium, Christensen brings together clothes by Paul & Joe from France, Matthew Williamson and Burberry from the UK, and Scandinavian labels such as Reykjavik. The overall look, complemented by Bruno Frisoni shoes and jewelry by Judi Frieman, is stylish, unusual and playful.

Vaucluse
Watsons Bay
Bondi
Bronte
Clovelly

Head east of Woollahra and it is all about beaches. On a sunny day it seems that all of Sydney is en route to Bondi and Bronte. Traffic is reduced to a slow crawl down Old South Head Road and Bondi Road, and parking spaces are as elusive as the meaning of life — which to many of the surfers waiting on the shores is the perfect wave. For all its international fame and glamour Bondi is, at times, reminiscent of Blackpool or Coney Island, a pleasure magnet for the masses. It's also a key pitstop on the world backpacker trail; stroll along Hall Street or Campbell Parade and it feels like you're in a fashion advertisement surrounded by sun-bronzed multi-ethnic youths with tattoos, body piercings and boardshorts all de rigueur. Recently, though, the beachside suburb has had a major sophistication injection courtesy of several high-profile restaurant and bar openings, including Icebergs (p. 140) and Moorish (p. 78) at either end of the beach and Mu Shu (p. 82) on Campbell Parade. Gould Street's row of boutiques (p. 78) is the place to hunt for the coolest designer jeans, T-shirts or sneakers.

Dominated by gargantuan apartment blocks and an unappealing shopping precinct (amongst the ugliest in Sydney) Bondi Junction, back towards the city, is also undergoing a partial makeover with the strikingly designed redevelopment of the Westfield shopping mall, scheduled to open in 2004.

Decent walking shoes come in handy for the spectacular cliff-top, shoreline walks that start at Bondi and head south towards Clovelly, providing sweeping views of the coast. Every October the highly recommended Sculpture by the Sea competition is held here. The beautiful people of Sydney spread their beach towels at Tamarama (a.k.a. Glamarama) while families and large groups of people head for Bronte. Clovelly, south of Waverley Cemetery, is more serene, its long narrow inlet ideal for snorkelling.

North of Bondi the harbour beaches dotted around the wealthy suburb of Vaucluse have a more exclusive atmosphere. The foreshore walks from Rose Bay around the craggy head will bring you to secluded Milk Beach, at the foot of Strickland House, with its amazing views across to the city, or you could have a blissful picnic at the strip of sand beside Vaucluse House (p. 78).

The crowds return at Watsons Bay, Sydney's first fishing village, with its famous hotel, fish-and-chip restaurant and café (p. 78). Escape by walking north to the lighthouse at the tip of South Head, passing the nudist Lady Bay Beach, or south towards the dramatic cliff-top plunge known as the Gap.

COLONIAL ESTATE

1 Vaucluse House
Wentworth Road

To get an idea of how rich landowners once lived in Sydney, visit Vaucluse House, home from 1827 to 1862 of William Charles Wentworth, a hugely influential Australian-born colonist. Apart from exploring Australia and forming its first university, he co-founded the colony's first independent newspaper, *The Australian*. The handsome Gothic revival–style house, with its shady, wisteria-draped verandahs and roof-top crenellations, now sits in verdant grounds of over 10 hectares; the original estate extended to 206 hectares. The Historic Houses Trust of News South Wales, who manage the property, have restored the gardens, gravel carriageways, picket fences and small farmyard at the back. Inside it's furnished as it would have been during Wentworth's time with European pieces including Bohemian glass and Meissen china.

FISH SUPPER

2 Watson Bay & Doyles
1 Military Road & 11 Marine Parade

When the Doyle family started serving fish suppers at Watson Bay in 1885, their guests arrived by horse and carriage or sailing cutter. Five generations later the Doyle family are still in residency at this picturesque bay 12 kilometres from Circular Quay, and most people get here by the State Transit ferry. Water taxi is also a good option, as is the very pleasant walk from Vaucluse House passing through secluded Parsley Bay with its mini suspension bridge. The original Doyle's restaurant is in the blue-and-white painted waterside building, but you can also enjoy their Manning and Hawkesbury River oysters, sand whiting, bream, barramundi and crayfish at the boisterous beer garden beside the Doyle's Palace Hotel, or at the outlet over the wharf. Alternatively, get a takeaway and avoid the crowds by wandering up the grassy slopes of Robertson Park behind. A couple of minutes walk away, the Pacific Ocean crashes at the foot of the awe-inspiring Gap, Sydney's most infamous suicide spot.

BONDI GROOVER

3 Brown Sugar

FOR ETERNITY

4 Remo

GOOD VIBRATIONS

5 Sean's Panaroma
139

MOROCCAN MIXES

6 Moorish
118–20 Ramsgate Avenue

Return Services League (RSL) clubs are found all over Sydney, and are best known for cheap drinks, cheaper food and clinking ranks of pokies (slot machines), rather than for having celebrity chefs, cocktail bars and sleek contemporary interiors. So when Luke Mangan and Lucy Allon of Salt fame (p. 135) took over the ground floor of the North Bondi RSL, it caused a stampede of the curious to the far northern end of Sydney's most famous beach, and the accolades have been pouring in. Moorish serves a clever mix of modern north African- and Spanish-influenced dishes and excellent cocktails – try the elderflower flavoured Martini for a drink that's like distilled springtime. The 28-year-old head chef, Perry Hill, worked at London's River Cafe before returning to his native Australia with lots of ideas about what to cook in a tagine and how best to use harissa, sumac and chermoula. It is one of the best places in Bondi for a lazy weekend brunch or late night drinks without the backpacker crowd.

GROOVY STREET

7 Gould Street
- Tuchuzy, no. 90
- Alfies, no. 85
- Electric Monkey, no. 78
- ...from St Xavier, no. 75a

'How groovy are you?' is the question painted on the mirror at the back of Tuchuzy (pronounced Too Choosy). Since you've found Gould Street, the hippest shopping strip in Bondi, the answer is very groovy indeed, thank you! Tuchuzy is one of the better boutiques found along this narrow street one block from the seafront. Alongside Paper, Denim and Cloth jeans and Adidas sneakers you'll find adorable baby-sized Chesty Bonds singlets in candy colours. Alfies stocks tsubi, G-star and Ringspun for both men and women, and Electric Monkeys mixes CDs and LPS into its street-fashion parade. A smattering of modern art and depictions of dramatically crashing waves on the walls, reminiscent of a Japanese woodblock print, at ...from St Xavier form a backdrop for womenswear by local labels Peni and Nooki among the imports from Italy (Freesoul jeans), the UK (Buddhist Punk and Religion) and South Korea (Minus Ung).

CUTIE PIE

8 Skipping Girl

124A Roscoe Street

The strong graphics and beach-babe look of Skipping Girl products are getting this local brand noticed. Designer Hayley Allen got her big idea for woven tote bags when she saw traditional shopping bags at a local market it southern India. The designs are fashioned from brightly coloured woven nylon and have a skipping rope handle – hence the label name. New bag designs are produced each season and they are now made in cotton and wool as well. They have been such a success that, five years on, Allen has expanded her range to cover bikinis, T-shirts, sweat tops and a range of accessories from belts to bobby pins. It's all cute, and fun and the fashion world from Barneys to Harvey Nichols now stocks the Skipping Girl range. See it all here first.

STYLE GOES TO THE BEACH

9 Ravesi's

LITERARY CONNECTION

10 Gertrude & Alice

40 Hall Street

Bondi's grooviest secondhand bookshop and café is named after Gertrude Stein and Alice B. Toklas. With piles of books covering a multitude of topics, comfy leather sofas and shared tables, it conjures up the bohemian spirit of early 20th-century Paris. You won't find Toklas's notorious hash cookies recipe on the menu but there are plenty of legal, delicious morsels to sample, including a meze plate for two, a lasagne just like your Italian mamma makes and a range of hearty soups in winter. Thanks to Bondi's transient population of international visitors it is also a good place to browse for foreign language books.

CRUSH ON YOU

11 Venetia Elaine/Icebirg

71 Hall Street

Sharing a boutique are the ethereal garments of Venetia Elaine and the glittery costume jewelry of Icebirg. Elaine's light and floaty dresses, tops and skirts are ideal for travellers, being made from silk organza, cotton and other natural fibres that are meant to have a crushed and un-ironed look. The clothes, which include maternity wear and childrenswear, are hand-dyed in a natural and dusty antique palate, including cream, pink and mauve as well as classic black and white. Sequins, shiny beads and silvery chains are all used in the inventive, colourful costume jewelry of designer and importer Birgit Moller.

HOME-MADE DELIGHTS

12 Green's Cafe

140 Glenayr Avenue

Who needs a view when you're sat in as cute a cafe as Green's? Painted a cool shade of peppermint, with walls covered in framed pictures, plates and knitted tea cosies, there's a nostalgic feel, like your granny's parlour, to the place – reinforced by the many homemade foods on offer. Jams, relishes, breads and nougat are all made and sold here by Sean's Panaroma alumnus Cathy Armstrong. Green's is big on breakfast. As well as the usual fry ups you can indulge in warm buttered peach and almond bread, cinnamon waffles with berries or grilled gruyere and asparagus on rye. For lunch, a popular option is the chunky steak sandwich with their sweet onion chutney, creamy garlic mayonnaise, roasted tomato and rocket.

SEVENTIES REVIVAL

13 Dragstar

96 Glenayr Avenue, shop 2

Celia Morris began designing clothes aged 12, during the 1970s. The spirit of that carefree era of chopper bikes, flares, funky patterns and everyday glamour infuses her fashion creations today. Girls who wouldn't know the Bay City Rollers from the Back Street Boys now crave her sassy orchid print T-shirts, polka-dot elasticated dresses and tube tops and chunky plastic bangles in snappy colours. Her range of leather bags is much admired – check out the 1980s–style shoulder bag in soft Italian leather. There's also a branch on King Street, Newtown.

SWEDISH FORMS

14 Funkis

23C Curlewis Street

The clean lines, organic forms and saturated colours of Swedish and Finnish homewares and furniture is Funkis's speciality. At their main outlet (they also have a branch in the Strand Arcade; p. 33) you can find pieces by Australian designers, including the cured hoop pine furniture of IYR (In Your Room) whose curvy, clever pieces began as children's furniture but have been taken up by the sophisticated adult design set. They also stock Florence Broadhurst printed fabric and wallpaper and some vintage mid-20th-century ceramics, glassware and furniture from Scandinavia and Australia.

15 Mu Shu

108 Campbell Parade

Hot on the heels of recent high-profile restaurant and bar openings in Bondi comes Mu Shu, a Shanghai dream of modern Asian dining that seems out of place amid the surf shops and tatty cafés of Campbell Parade. Not that it matters once you step inside and sink onto one of the red upholstered daybeds or perch on one of the wire mesh stools by Philippine designer Ann Pamintuan. American Michael McCann is responsible for the dazzling interior with its exposed brick walls and metal trusses, discrete rear booths padded with saffron-coloured silk and Indonesian silver objet d'art on the wall. Mirroring the nine-metre-long bar is the open kitchen, the centre piece of which is the Chinese duck roasting oven. New Zealand chef Dean Kendell's other specialities include delicious soy-and-black-vinegar lacquered baby chicken or barbecued lamb rack with taro cakes. A decent cocktail and wine list, with several good choices by the glass, all adds to the appeal.

BONDI CLASSIC

16 Hugo's

70 Campbell Parade

Long before Icebergs, Moorish and Mu Shu swept into Bondi on a wave of high-fashion and dining glamour, intimate and chic Hugo's was the place to see and be seen. It's still a classy performer, having set the standard for beachside dining with its stylish interior of leather upholstered benches, plump yellow and sailor blue cushions and famous painting of a blue-faced man poking himself in the eye. The food is as relaxed, handsome and tasty as the décor: vine-ripened tomatoes stuffed with caramelized goat curd and served with crisp olive bread and tapenade; pan-seared king prawns with an avocado and roast capsicum salad; blue-swimmer-crab linguine; or crisply fried tea-smoked duck breast. The outdoor seats are popular with those who don't wish to miss any of the comings and goings on Campbell Parade.

LOCATION, LOCATION, LOCATION!

17 Icebergs Dining Room & Bar

140

THE LOOK OF THE LAND

18 Cloth

166

THE FAMILY BEACH

19 Bronte

- Sejuced, 487 Bronte Road
- Maverick, 471 Bronte Road

A sweep of sand not as long as Bondi but bigger than Tamarama, a broad expanse of grass dotted with public barbecue pits and a toy train for kids mark out Bronte as the perfect family beach. There's also some great cafés, including the long-running Sejuced known for its freshly pressed juices, cakes and coffees. The newcomer is Maverick, which outshines the rest in terms of design – the brown leather banquettes and deep red walls are more nightclub than beachside caff. But their breakfast menu of sticky black rice, palm sugar, coconut cream and mango or toasted brioche with strawberries is rather fancy too.

GENTLEMAN'S RETREAT

20 Bronte House

470 Bronte Road

Open to the public six days a year (check the website for details), Bronte House was built in 1844 by architect Mortimer Lewis, the man responsible for Government House in the Royal Botanical Gardens. It is one of the oldest buildings in the eastern suburbs, and the only surviving colonial house in New South Wales to overlook the ocean. The house – a *cottage orné* with Gothic touches – has a very English feel, but it is the 1.8 hectare gardens, with a native shrubbery merging naturally with the adjoining Bronte Gully that lend it a romantic distinction. Restored and replanted with over 1500 plant varieties during the recent tenancy of Sydney arts supremo Leo Schofield, they include plants such as lilly pilly, as well as 16 dwarf date palms and 40 types of fragrant frangipani.

SNORKEL REQUIRED

21 Seasalt

1 Donnellan Circuit

If you follow the coastal path south from Bronte through atmospheric Waverley cemetery, resting place of writer and poet Henry Lawson, you'll eventually drop down into the narrow, sandy inlet of Clovelly. The sheltered position makes an ideal place to sunbathe, swim and snorkel should the waves be too strong on more exposed areas of the coast. Drop by Seasalt, a café designed by Burley Katon Halliday beneath the lifesaving club overlooking the beach. Settle into a lemon Jasper Morrison chair and enjoy simply prepared, tasty seafood dishes, such as beer-battered flathead, grilled bream or chili salt squid.

Inner West
Suburbs

Maybe it is their lack of studied hipness and a prediliction for shabby chic over high-concept contemporary style that give Sydney's inner-west suburbs their distinctive appeal. Spiralling house prices to the east have brought an influx of cash rich, upwardly mobile people to areas such as Newtown and Glebe, where impecunious students and alternative lifestylers previously held sway. The period architecture of Annandale, in particular, is prized for providing more space and better conditions than the real estate of Paddington or Darlinghurst. These communities are more spread out than others in the book, but over several days they can be explored on foot as easily and rewardingly.

Next to the University of Sydney, Glebe is an eclectic combination of handsome Victorian mansions and public housing. Its working-class roots are still in evidence — it is home to the Wentworth Park dog-racing track and Harold Park Raceway for harness racing. Glebe Point Road (p.88) is its main artery and a place to browse for secondhand books, cheap ethnic food and a bargain at the Saturday flea and crafts market. Also in the western precincts of the University, Newtown has a collegiate vibe. The suburb is synonymous with frenetic King Street (p.88), one of the longest continuous commercial strips in Sydney, filled with bookshops, homeware stores and Thai restaurants. Duck into the quiet side streets to discover green patches of parkland and pretty old churches, such as St Stephens on Church Street, where Charles Dickens found inspiration for *Great Expectations*.

Noisy and polluted Parramatta Road is the highway from which to access Annandale and Leichhardt, the main Italian quarter of Sydney, named after the German explorer who disappeared while exploring north Australia in 1848 and who was the inspiration for Nobel Prize-winning author Patrick White's book, *Voss*.

North of here, the monumental Anzac Bridge leads to the isolated suburbs of Rozelle and Balmain. Darling Street is the main thoroughfare, starting in Rozelle and dropping steeply to the harbour at the East Balmain ferry wharf. Named after William Balmain, a ship's surgeon in the First Fleet who was granted land rights to the peninsula in 1800, this inner-city village was, for most of its history, a base for mining and maritime industries — the Australian Labour Party was founded in one of the area's many pubs. Over the years Balmain has morphed from a faintly bohemian, working-class suburb into one inhabited by media stars and professionals on six-figure incomes who find its sandstone and wrought-iron architecture particularly appealing.

1 Glebe Point Road
- Badde Manors, no. 37
- Glebe Market
- Gleebooks, no. 49
- Valhalla, no. 166

Cyber cafés, recycled clothing, CD- and bookstores and cheap ethnic eateries follow each other down the student hub, starting with the ever reliable Badde Manors; for 20 years this corner café, with its cosy wooden booths, Déco–style lamps and stylish espresso machine, has been selling caffeine fixes, lentil and tofu burgers, delectable cakes and home-made ice cream to the student masses. Saturday is the day to visit so you can drop by the craft and junk market in front of Glebe Public School. Opposite is Gleebooks, one of the street's best bookstores (they have a secondhand branch further up the hill, which also specializes in children's books). Valhalla, although looking decidedly past its Art Déco best, is a movie-going institution. There's still a lot of charm to this cinema, and you've got to admire it for resolutely sticking to an uncommercial programme of documentaries and esoteric art-house flicks.

ANTIQUE STYLE

2 Tricketts

| 126 |

BAYSIDE APHRODISIAC

3 The Boathouse Blackwattle Bay

| 142 |

CERAMIC ART

4 Mura Clay Gallery
49–51 King Street

Seeing a gap in Sydney's art market for contemporary ceramics and sculptures, Irene Mura Schroder started this gallery in 1990. Plenty have followed her lead, but Mura Clay Gallery remains one of the best places to sample some of the most interesting three-dimensional art work in Australia. On display are functional, organically shaped platters and plates by David Edmunds, more decorative and intriguingly glazed vases by Merran Esson and flattened vases and pitchers by Gillian Brionowski, which bridge the gap between the pottery of Mura's usual collection and its recent exhibition of two-dimensional works and paintings. Lisa Roberts's Antarctica-inspired works in perspex, which look like carved ice blocks, take the gallery in another interesting direction.

CAFFEINE CHAMPIONS

5 Campos
193 Missenden Road

This shrine to the art of coffee making draws disciples from all over the inner west for its fresh brews, best sipped while reading the morning paper at one of the seats by the windows. It's a tiny space cluttered with all manner of grinders, plungers and coffee-making paraphernalia, and one wall lined with vats for 18 varieties of coffee bean from around the world, including certified organic coffee from East Timor. Apart from a Belgium chocolate or friand, there's nothing to nibble, ensuring delicate coffee aromas are not spoilt by the smell of food. If you don't fancy coffee, their hot chocolate is also pretty good.

SPLIT PERSONALITY

6 King Street
- Goulds Book Arcade, nos 32–38
- T2, no. 173
- Pentimento, no. 249
- Oishi, no. 355
- Newtown Old Wares, no. 439
- Faster Pussycat, no. 431A
- Bank Hotel, no. 324

There are two distinct halves to King Street, the traffic clogged main artery of Newtown running for 2 kilometres from the edge of Sydney University to the tip of Sydney Park and the start of the Princes Highway. The change in consumer direction happens at the bend by Newtown train station. Secondhand bookstores dominate the eastern end, with the chaotic Goulds taking the prize for Sydney's most frustratingly messy book depository. Continue west to T2, a gourmet tea shop selling an impressive range of loose teas, herbal infusions, teapots and tea-making implements. Pentimento is a stylish gift, card and bookshop specializing in volumes on art, food and interior design – handy since the approaching second half of King Street focuses on homeware and furniture stores. Oishi stocks contemporary handmade teak furniture, mood-enhancing lamps and fluffy retro-style cushions. For real retro goodies, though, Newtown Old Wares offers 20th-century design gems from 'Déco to disco', as they put it – Tretchikoff prints look down over funky larva lamps and 1950s TV sets turned into fish tanks. The fabulously named Faster Pussycat has trashy pop culture books, clothing and accessories. Apart from all this, King Street is famous for Thai food – 17 restaurants at the last count. A good one can be found hidden in a fairy-light illuminated garden behind the Bank Hotel next to Newtown Station.

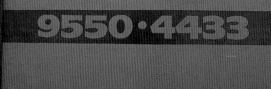

MURA
CLAY
GALLERY

CONTEMPORARY AUSTRALIAN CERAMICS
POTTERY SUPPLIES

9550·4433

7 Pretty Dog
1A Brown Street

Nothing for your pet pooch, but plenty of clothes for girls (and occasionally guys) who are looking to stay ahead of the mainstream fashion crowd. Tanya Stevanovic kept the name of the vintage clothing store she took over in 1997 but ditched the stock in favour of contemporary fashion from cutting-edge Australian and New Zealand designers. This cream and royal purple painted boutique and art gallery stocks Karen Walker and Justin Taylor, both of whose ranges span from T-shirts to suits. Nicola Finetti's garments are elegant and casual in silks and cotton, while the Lover label utilizes vintage Swedish cotton prints in its designs.

LIFE'S A DRAG

8 Erskineville Road
- Imperial Hotel, no. 35
- Big Boys Giftshop & Cafe, no. 106
- Rose of Australia Hotel, 1 Swanson Street

The Mardi Gras parade float workshops have recently vacated their premises on Erskineville Road, but the neighbourhood (known locally as Erko) is still famous for the eternal home of drag, The Imperial Hotel. This Art-Déco beauty, which gained international fame in *Priscilla: Queen of the Desert*, hosts hugely enjoyable, twisted drag shows every Thursday, Friday and Saturday night that take their themes from movies such as *The Sound of Music* and *One Flew Over the Cuckoo's Nest*, while host Mitzy Mackintosh keeps proceedings rolling in glitzy, high-kicking fashion. Perfect after a long night at the Imperial is gay-friendly Bigboys Giftshop Cafe, which doesn't really stock many gifts but does do a mean beefburger and breakfast fry up. Over the road, at the point where Erskineville Road turns into Swanson Street, the mood changes at the swanky, renovated pub The Rose of Australia, where actor Russell Crowe has been spotted having a drink. There's a very convivial restaurant upstairs and often live music at weekends in the saloon bar.

GOTHIC GLAMOUR

9 Enmore Road
- Emma's on Liberty, 59 Liberty Street
- Enmore Theatre, no. 130
- Gallery Serpentine, no. 123

Like nearby King Street, Enmore Road has many Thai restaurants, as well as a few decent Lebanese ones. The

best is Emma's on Liberty, a short walk away, which offers a fine range of classics from the Levant served in a convivial communal setting. Many people venture into the area to attend a concert at the Art Déco Enmore Theatre, where the Stones played one of their most intimate concerts since the 1960s when they visited in 2003. If you're looking for a suitably punk or rock n'roll outfit, Gallery Serpentine is dedicated to all things gothic, from lacy black corsets to Mr Darcy–style frock coats and jackets in velvet or leather.

LA DOLCE VITA

10 Norton Street

- The Merchant of Venice, Italian Forum
- WildEast Dreams, no. 102
- Sydney Gourmet Burger, no. 172
- Bar Italia, no. 169–71
- Elio, no. 159
- Berkelouw's Books, no. 70
- Norton Street Cinema, no. 99

The epicentre of Leichhardt is Norton Street, best visited on a weekend evening when it seems the whole Italian-dominated suburb comes out to eat, drink and socialize. At the Parramatta Road end is the terracotta and cream painted Italian Forum, a shopping and apartment complex designed to mimic the communal housing of the old country. Although residents are banned from hanging out washing on their balconies (as they most likely would in Italy) la dolce vita is laid on with a trowel: the boutiques stock Giorgio Armani and Versace, there's a statue of Dante by the gurgling fountain and many central courtyard cafés – none of them as good as they could be. The most interesting of the Forum's shops is The Merchant of Venice, which stocks a beautiful array of authentic gilded and painted Venetian masks and marionettes. Back on the street the general hegemony of Italian restaurants and cafés is being broken up by newcomers such as WildEast Dreams, serving spicey Malaysian and Indonesian food in a charming, gallery setting, and the ultra-slick Sydney Gourmet Burger. Across the road is the old standard Bar Italia, well known for its delicious gelato, and the starkly sophisticated Elio, about the best Italian restaurant on the street. Norton Street isn't all about eating and sipping an espresso. Berkelouw's is an excellent new, secondhand and rare bookshop (with a pleasant café), and the Norton Street Cinema screens the pick of independent and art movies in Sydney, as well as hosting an annual festival of Italian cinema.

藍薑

Blue Ginger

241

BELLE FLEUR

LONDON HOTEL

11 The Essential Ingredient
4 Australia Street

This enormous kitchen supplies shop, patronized by almost every chef in Sydney for their comprehensive stock of professional and domestic cookware, is well worth a detour along Parramatta Road. From cake moulds and cook pots to terracotta tagines and knives, they're bound to have it – and in a myriad shapes and sizes. The range of cookbooks, many by top Sydney chefs, is particularly impressive. There is a section of gourmet foods and difficult to find ingredients, such as Persian fairy floss (a great alternative to spun toffee) and spicy wasabi oil from Japan.

SUBURBAN BLISS
12 Three Clicks West
142

BLARNEY CHARMER
13 The Welcome Hotel
148

SWEET SCULPTURES
14 Belle Fleur
658 Darling Street

Three generations of chocolate makers in the Ter Heerdt family are behind this confectionary shop that, since 1984, has established itself as one of the best in Sydney. The chocolates are made daily on the premises, guaranteeing their freshness, and no preservatives, artificial colours or additives are used. Their speciality is ones filled with whipped creams, and, as well as the usual fillings like caramel, hazelnut and macadamia paste, they produce uniquely Australian flavours such as wattleseed and lemon myrtle. Their chocolate making is a real art, as demonstrated by the many inventive moulded shapes, such as mobile phones, clowns and violins and mouthwatering window displays at Easter and Christmas.

ALL OVER ASIA
15 Blue Ginger
241 Darling Street

The salt-and-pepper chili squid always gets the thumbs up at this buzzy Balmain Asian-fusion restaurant. The high-ceilinged room is big and open but also warm and stylishly decorated. Owner and chef Leslie Huynh is not afraid to fuse Thai salads, Malaysian laksas, Mongolian lamb and Japanese tempura on the same menu – it's a credit to him that, for the most part, it works. They usually have barramundi cooked in a variety of ways – try it with ginger, shallot and oyster sauce. Interesting desserts and an extensive, good value wine list make this one of the area's better dining experiences.

DAWN WAS HERE
16 Darling Street
• London Hotel, no. 234
• The Monkey Bar, no. 255
• Punch Gallery, no. 209
• Suyu Emporium, no. 303
• Johnston & Bell, no. 364
• Gosh, no. 297
• Balmain & Rozelle Markets
• Canteen, no. 332
• Mofo, no. 354

The old maritime neighbourhood of Balmain was known for having the greatest concentration of pubs of any Sydney suburb. Quite a few can still be found along Darling Street – many of them boasting a connection to Balmain's favourite daughter, the Olympic medal-winning swimmer Dawn Fraser. For a contrast of old and new Balmain, kick off at the London Hotel where you can perch on an iron tractor stool on the outdoor balcony, then move on to the contemporary stylings of the Monkey Bar with its dark blue leather seating and gourmet pub grub. Opposite the London Hotel is the intriguing Punch Gallery, a jewelry and objet d'art gallery where you can find beaded creations by Alisa McCabe and Rebecca Bruhm's cloth sculptures. Costume jewelry in extravagant European designs are the stock-in-trade of glamourous boutique Suyu – owner Su Yu has trawled the world for dresses, shoes and accessories for over 18 years. More beads and sequins can be found at Johnston & Bell, but their speciality is sheer slip dresses with lace and floral ribbon trims. Gosh promises 'things to die for', which is maybe going a little overboard on the appeal of its camp consumables such as Betty Boop ceramics, masks and feather boas. The street is bookended by two weekend crafts and bric-à-brac markets. The arty Balmain market is in the grounds of St Andrew's Church every Saturday; the Rozelle market at Rozelle Public School, happens on Saturday and Sunday. The street's best café is Canteen with its high ceilings, communal and pavement tables; they bake the French bread used in their sandwiches on the premises. Pink and gold painted Mofo goes in for funkier 1950s décor. There's always a quote of the day (for example: 'Love takes time') to go with their lemon poppy seed muffins or stack of corn and parsley fritters.

North Shore

'Seven miles from Sydney and a thousand miles from care,' is Manly's well-worn catchphrase. Although Sydneysiders are tired of hearing this, Manly — named by the first colonial Governor Arthur Phillip after the 'manly' Aboriginal people he spotted on the shore — does have the distinct atmosphere of a seaside resort. The feeling of separateness from Sydney is reinforced if you sail here on a double decker ferry from Circular Quay — one of the best ways to see the spectacular views along the length of Sydney Harbour.

It is only a five minute stroll across Manly from the ferry terminal on Manly Cove, with its tranquil harbourside beaches, to the Norfolk Pine fringed sweep of golden sand where surf waves crash in from the Pacific. Linking the two sides is the Corso, Manly's principal shopping boulevard and another testament to Sydney's love of the Art-Déco façade. There is always something going on, be it a surfing or scuba diving class at the beach, where many a local sporting hero has trained, or mums meeting up along the Corso for a mid-morning coffee. With all the day-trippers, surfers and backpackers (it's a favourite British holiday haunt) Manly can be, at times, a rather tacky, commercial scene. It also used to be a much earlier to bed kind of place than Sydney, but that's beginning to change with the opening of the hip Manly Wharf Hotel (p. 147) and several café—bars along the South Steyne. A few good shops and boutiques, some stocking the artfully distressed jeans of local design collective tsubi, are also worth hunting out.

Elsewhere the well-heeled harbourside suburbs of Sydney's North Shore are uniformly wonderful, leafy places to live, if you can afford a multi-million dollar family home and have a hankering for a quiet and conservative lifestyle, a thousand miles from the hullabaloo of the city. Beneath the Harbour Bridge at Milson's Point, the clown face at the entrance to newly re-opened Luna Park seems to be mocking those on the southern shore who believe all life ends at Circular Quay. A trip along Military Road, the major thoroughfare winding its way east from North Sydney through Neutral Bay and Cremorne towards Mosman, throws up several unique pleasures, particularly at Balmoral Beach, one the most seductive destinations in Sydney, as does the neighbourhood of Castlecrag, further to the north.

The real attraction of a visit to this side of Sydney, though, is the opportunity to look back at the city from some of the harbour's most propitious stretches of parkland. Come here to walk from Spit Bridge at the east end of Mosman to Manly, a hike running through terrain almost unchanged since Arthur Phillip sailed into the harbour over 200 years ago.

WONDER POOL

1 North Sydney Olympic Pool

- Ripples
- Aqua Dining

Next to the grotesquely huge grinning clown face at the entrance to Luna Park is the glorious Art Déco North Sydney Olympic Pool. Built on the site where much of the construction work for the Sydney Harbour Bridge was done, it was hailed the 'wonder pool of Australasia' when it opened in 1936 because of its excellent facilities and sophisticated modern filtration system. After a recent $10 million upgrade the pool, in which 86 world records have been set, still amazes. Nowhere else can you swim in an open-air 50-metre heated pool with a view of the Harbour Bridge spanning magnificently above. The facility now has a 25-metre indoor pool, gym, spa, sauna and a couple of decent places to eat. Ripples is a casual café where you can snack on French toast or muesli after your morning workout, or grab a Szechuan spiced tuna and green mango salad. The glass-walled Aqua Dining, housed in the pool's old caretaker's quarters, is expense account territory, offering classy mod-Oz tucker for lunch and dinner.

FISH CAFÉ

2 Garfish

2/21 Broughton Street

This superior fish-and-chip café, run by the former owners of nearby Milsons, and with young talent Damian Heads in the kitchen, is a casual breakfast-to-dinner place that could hardly go wrong. As well as all the usual suspects, Garfish serves up some more unusual seafood such as bar cod or skate. Six different fish are listed each day with a suggested cooking method and accompaniment. The friendly waiters will give you advice, but essentially it's up to you. They make their own Belgium waffles to go with fancy ice creams, brew a mean coffee and have outdoor seating. The Kirribilli residents know a good thing when they see it, so expect to wait at peak meal times.

PRE-THEATRE PLEASURE

3 Milsons

17 Willoughby Street

Just up the road from the waterside Ensemble Theatre, Sydney's longest running professional theatre company, is the equally venerable and reliable Milsons. Chef Lee Kweiz is the latest to take up residency in this sleek, contemporary restaurant with sultry lighting, padded walls and rustic décor. He describes his food as 'fresh

Australian', which is putting a spin on the usual mod-Oz tag, but is a fair description of a menu that reflects the season's best produce. Meals are bookended by an amuse-gueule and petit fours, adding a formal touch to what is always a pleasant gastronomic experience.

PAN-ASIAN EATERY

4 Temple
165 Wycombe Road

A hit from the word go, Temple has brought communal dining and pan-Asian cuisine to an area of the North Shore better known for its Japanese restaurants. This is a very sophisticated space with sinuous Chinese calligraphy on the walls, a Bodhisattva on the open kitchen counter, incense coils and polished floorboards. No big surprises on the menu, but it is well cooked and keenly priced. You could start with a temple sampler for two of grilled prawns, fish cakes, rice paper rolls and chicken saté. Seafood includes barramundi grilled with ginger and shallots or chili-and-black-bean sauce. The noodle options take their inspiration from Singapore to Vietnam via Thailand.

LITTLE CHARMER

5 Chaos Café
194 Military Road

You have to work hard on the drinks, food and charm when you're a café facing a car park and hidden away at the rear of a bland shopping complex on the Neutral Bay section of Military Road. Chaos Café manages this with ease. The mosaic floor and brightly painted chairs that could have been pinched from one of the area's trendy daycare centres are immediately appealing. Fruits whips are a delicious vitamin C rich alternative to their zingy caffeine fixes. Breakfast, which includes traditional choices and the more unusual 'breakie wrap', scrambled eggs with smoked salmon and a sprinkling of chili in a flour tortilla, is served until the very civilized time of 3.30 pm.

BORN TO SHOP

6 Military Road
- The Hayden Orpheum Picture Palace, no. 380
- Red Gum Restaurant Bar, no. 624
- Grain Interior, no. 527
- Trilogie, no. 587
- Country Road, no. 742

There's no shortage of shopping opportunities further down Military Road, especially as the busy highway narrows and drops down towards Taronga Zoo. The most

interesting are after the fork with Spit Road, but before then there are a handful of places to pause. The splendid Art-Déco Cremorne Hayden Orpheum Picture Palace is a six-screen cinema dating from 1935, complete with an illuminated Wurlitzer organ that rises out of the stage pit of the main auditorium before weekend evening shows. They sometimes have special screenings of classic movies to complement the graceful majesty of the cinema, which has been renovated. Another heritage building being put to good use is Boronia House, dating from 1885 and set back from the road in pretty gardens. A popular location for weddings, it is occupied by the restaurant and bar Red Gum, which specializes in using native Australian ingredients such as kangarooo, barramundi, bush tomato and wattleseeds in its Asian-influenced dishes. Across the road the East-meets-West furniture and homewares of Grain Interior are a study in the relaxed living aesthetic of the North Shore. A more romantic French provincial style is available at Trilogie where you can find vintage and reproduction goods – from an antique bed to a 1950s ironing board. Few stores do chic contemporary living – in fashion, homewares and furniture – as well as Country Road, the national chain store that has a spacious outlet in the attractive old Anzac Memorial Hall.

BRIGHT YOUNG FASHION

7 You Never Know
5 Spit Road, shop 3

Fashion tends to cater to the more conservative, older woman at this end of town, but one place offering something attractive for younger customers is Stephanie Fengles's You Never Know. Stocking beach-girl chic brands such as Wish, Bebe and the edgy urban streetwear of One Teaspoon, she aims to offer everything from casual and office wear to evening and swimwear. Matching belts, bags, shoes and jewelry make it a one-stop shop that's surprisingly affordable.

CENTRAL-AMERICAN JOE

8 Don Adán Coffee House

BURLEY GRIFFIN'S VISION

9 Castlecrag
• Lunch
• Simon Johnson

One of North Sydney's prettiest suburbs is Castlecrag, a testament to the vision of its principal architect, Walter Burley Griffin. The American architect and his wife,

Marion, arrived in Australia in 1912, having won the competition to design the new national capital Canberra. After Griffin resigned from the project in 1920, he turned his attention to developing 263 hectares of land in Middle Harbour into an estate that was in harmony with nature. There were to be no fences or boundaries, and homes were orientated towards communal parks landscaped with native flora. Although the ideals and covenants that originally protected the area have gone, something of Griffin's utopian vision remains. This is where you'll find Sydney's Rudolph Steiner school, and a walk down Edinburgh Road towards the tip of the promintory reveals some fine houses, including seven by Griffin.

The low-key shopping centre at the junction of Edinburgh Road and Eastern Valley Way is home to Annie Parmentier's Lunch, one of those hidden away restaurant secrets you'll be tempted to keep to yourself. It is open for breakfast, lunch and occasionally dinner, and always serves something special. Wide canvas umbrellas provide shelter as you tuck into dishes from the daily changing blackboard menu covering all bases from fresh fish and homemade gnocchi to delectable desserts. Next door, confirming the suburb's affluence and good taste, is a branch of quality providore Simon Johnson (p. 37).

ZOO WITH A VIEW

10 Taronga Zoo
Bradleys Head Road

Having seen cuddly koala and kangaroo toys in tourist shops all over Sydney, view the real thing at this park occupying 30 hectares of prime harbourside real estate above Bradleys Head. If arriving by ferry from Circular Quay, it's a good idea to take the bus to the grand main entrance dating from 1916 when the zoo first opened and work your way back downhill through the many enclosures. The Australian Walkabout area allows you to get up close to kangaroos and wallabies, and, although you can no longer cuddle a koala, you can have your photo taken beside one. 4000 other creatures, including more native fauna such as the nocturnal platypus and frill-necked lizard, share the leafy space. The new Backyard to Bush exhibit navigates a fascinating journey from the familiar animals and insects found in Australian homes, including menacing redback spiders, a giant wombat burrow typical of the bush, and slugs in a farmyard mailbox! Work is underway on new attractions, including a walk through rainforest home for Asian elephants and a Great Southern Oceans mega-display. Every summer popular concerts are held in the zoo at twilight.

11 Athol Hall & Bradleys Head

Bradleys Head Road

Sydney Harbour National Park begins down the hill from the zoo. Just within the park entrance, off Bradleys Head Road, you'll find Athol Hall, little more than a weatherboard building painted in heritage colours housing an infrequently opened café. Sitting on the hall's verandah, sipping a reviving cup of tea and watching rabbits bounce on the neatly clipped lawn, you'll quickly realize why this is a favourite spot for North Shore weddings. The uninterrupted vista through to the city is breathtaking, as are the views from the tip of the head, named after Lieutenant William Bradley, a cartographer on the First Fleet. There's added foreground interest in the form of the land-mounted mast of H.M.A.S. Sydney, a First World War battleship that sunk the German raider Emden in 1914, and – in the water – one of the six original Doric columns that formed part of the portico of Sydney's General Post Office until it was demolished in 1863. A path runs from here to Taylors Bay, Clifton Gardens and the small beach and ocean baths at Chowder Bay.

BEACHSIDE CHIC
12 Bathers' Pavilion Restaurant & Cafe

143

BALMORAL MINIMALISM
13 Awaba

67 The Esplanade

The Bathers' Pavilion is full? No worries, mate. Awaba is just across the road. The stripped back, minimalist décor couldn't be more of a contrast to that of the plush, beach-bohemian Bathers'. Gleaming white walls and chairs, a concrete island bar, concertina windows and expansive mirrors – it is a stark canvas enlivened by happy customers and perky black-clad staff. And who wouldn't be happy when they serve simple, good classics such as a crisp caesar salad with grilled chicken or rocket tossed with smoked salmon and cucumber. For dinner try their scotch fillet with creamy mashed potato and garlic confit.

INNER-CITY BUSHWALK
14 The Spit to Manly walk

• Fresh Ketch
• Afternoon Harbour Cruise

The 10-kilometre trail from the Spit Bridge to Manly passes through pristine native bushland, ancient Aboriginal sites and harbourside suburbs and beaches. At a steady pace it will take three-to-four hours to walk, but you could easily spend a whole day exploring the various off-route tracks and lingering at the beautiful beaches along the way; Forty Baskets Beach is particularly nice. A great variety of wildlife can be spotted in the parkland, including lizards, possums and rainbow lorikeets high up in the Sydney Red Gums that shade part of the route. Refreshments are available at either end of the walk; try the seafood at Fresh Ketch at Spit Bridge or revive with a schooner and some oysters at the Manly Wharf Hotel (p. 147). There's usually an ice-cream van at the lookout over Crater Cove. Alternatively, you can view this side of the harbour on the two-and-a-half-hour State Transit Afternoon Harbour Cruise, which departs from Circular Quay (1 pm weekdays; 1.30 pm weekends) and sails under the opening Spit Bridge into Middle Harbour.

SEASIDE SOPHISTICATE
15 Manly Wharf Hotel

147

BAG TO THE FIFTIES
16 Glamourpuss

169

ART & FASHION
17 Spacejunk

164

NOT THE CORSO
18 Pittwater Road

• Peter Mitchell Jewellery
• Pulp

Pittwater Road is where Manly abandons the slavish devotion to chain stores found along the Corso and discovers its own shopping identity. After you've got your hip outfit from boutique Spacejunk, accessorize the look with Peter Mitchell's chunky jewelry. He's been designing and hand-making jewelry for over 15 years, cementing his reputation for heavy silver pieces like his chain link bracelets and necklaces as well as work in yellow, black, rose and white gold. Rings are studded in a range of semi-precious stones, including tourmalines, amethysts and aquamarines. If you want to package your purchases with unusual wrapping paper and cards, then walk down the road to Pulp. Owner Margaret Rockliff has assembled a collection of papers made from, among other things, cotton, sugarcane, silk and indigenous seeds.

19 Ground Zero

18 Sydney Road, shop 2

Manly is not particularly well served with classy cafés but Ground Zero makes up for the deficit by providing a fine range of coffees and teas, as well as more than palatable snacks, in a stylish, comfortable environment. Their range of teas – black, green, white, oolong, organic, flavoured, herbal infusions – is impressive. It's worth dropping by for the chance to sample unusual brews such as lapacho vanilla, made from the inner bark of the lapacho tree of the high Andes, or black tea flavoured with Australian lemon myrtle. Their freshly baked muffins are the business, and their courtyard a quiet place to relax away from the beachside bustle.

SURF DE LUXE

20 Surfection

82–86 The Corso

To see how far surf shops have evolved since the days of niche retailing into the broader world of street fashion, pay a visit to the dazzling Surfection, the largest surfwear shop in the country. This flagship store of the big chain has been given a glitzy Rodeo Drive–style makeover by Ian Halliday of Burley, Katon, Halliday. Out go the bright lights and even brighter colours usually associated with surf shops, and in comes a warm palate of stone, timber and calm, soft illumination. All the major brands – Billabong, Mambo, Quiksilver – are stocked and, if you really want to, amid all the boardshorts, jeans, T-shirts and sneakers, you can buy a surfboard too.

NORDIC LOUNGE

21 Manly Ocean Beach House

Ocean Promenade, South Steyne

The one-time information kiosk on South Steyne promenade has been given a Scandinavian chic makeover to turn it into the Manly Ocean Beach House. The dining room and bar – all soft lighting, blonde wood furniture and floorboards – sits up high allowing an unbroken view through the fringe of Norfolk Pines towards the breaking surf. It's certainly the most stylish place along a very commercial strip, popular with the surfing and backpacking crowd. Open from breakfast to dinner, they serve Australian cuisine with a European inflection, so you may find pan-roasted kangaroo in a heady port sauce alongside crispy battered fish and hand-cut chips. There's a good selection of German beers and cocktails should you just wish to kick back and enjoy the beachside panorama into the night.

BEACHSIDE MAGIC

22 Le Kiosk

1 Marine Parade

Follow the eco-sculpture walk from Manly Surf Club at the southern end of Manly beach around Cabbage Tree Bay to calm Shelly Beach. It's one of Sydney's most delightful patches of sand – a place to snorkel and swim in ocean water without worrying about the waves. No need to bother about bringing a picnic either with Le Kiosk, one of Sydney's longest running restaurants, nestling in the shade of the trees a mere hop, skip and a jump from the sand. The sandstone cottage with navy blue painted woodwork and open fireplace strikes the right nautical note, and their menu embraces a variety of oysters, seared scallops and crispy skinned John Dory. The seafood platter at weekends is a popular way to justify a long lunch or dinner. In the evening, with fairy lights twinkling in the trees and the waves lapping gently on the beach, the location couldn't feel more magical.

GHOSTS OF THE PAST

23 Quarantine Station

North Head Scenic Drive

South of the neat streets of Manly the land rises up and juts out in a bulbous knuckle towards North Head, a wild and gothic area. The best views of the harbour are from the lookout points along the Fairfax Walking Track. There's a military reserve with the National Artillery Museum too but, more interesting – and revealing of Australia's recent history – is the old Quarantine Station on the harbour side. From 1832 to 1984 ships carrying passengers who had, or who were suspected of having, infectious diseases were obliged to dock here. On arrival, passengers and crew were quarantined for weeks. Approximately 570 people died here and legend has it that a few unquiet souls linger around the abandoned accommodation and shower blocks, hospital and mortuary. The station is run by the National Parks and Wildlife Service, and you have to book a guided tour to visit. If you've got the nerve for it, the ghost tours held at night from Friday to Sunday add an extra level of atmospherics to an already spooky place.

sleep

In a city where everyone would prefer to be cruising the sun-dappled streets or lazing on the beach, it's not surprising that hotels have tended to neglect their décor and have not invested in their own style. This is beginning to change, as the following selection shows. Although not yet on a par with London or New York, in Sydney it is entirely possible to avoid corporate hotel blandness and find accommodation with character and individuality – from a charming bed and breakfast with the warmest of welcomes to chic and glitzy boudoirs fit for visiting pop glitterati.

THE GRAND DAME

14 **The Observatory Hotel**

4 89–113 Kent Street
Rooms from $360

A short stroll uphill from Circular Quay, the opulently colonial and supremely well mannered Observatory Hotel stands out among Sydney's premier league of luxury hotels. The old-world charm of the 96-room establishment, with elegant furnishings, an outstanding range of facilities and staff who make every guest feel like royalty, is apparent the moment you step inside.

The antique character of yesteryear is played up in the heritage district of the Rocks and The Orient-Express group, who run the hotel, know their market and are happy to cater to such expectations. The quality of what they provide is self-evident – rooms come with DVD and CD players as well as cable television and broadband Internet access, while historic Australian landscape prints and Asian ceramics add an exotic touch. The muted colour schemes and plush furnishings conspire to create an aura of exquisite refinement.

If you want extra space there are eight junior suites and 12 executive suites, some with four poster beds. Views are towards the working port area of Walsh Bay on one side and across to Observatory Hill on the other .

The day spa and health club is one the best at any of Sydney's hotels – you can swim backstroke in a 20-metre pool kept at a constant 28° Celsius while gazing up at a ceiling twinkling with a star map of the southern constellation. A nice bonus for all overseas guests is a free 30-minute session in the spa's flotation tank – a great way to deal with jet lag.

There are plenty of excellent restaurants and pubs in the Rocks but should you choose to stay in the hotel you certainly won't miss out. The Observatory's modern Australian restaurant Galileo is headed by Harunobu Inukai, a talented chef whose ambitious Restaurant VII sent Sydney foodies into raptures. The clubby Globe Bar is also a classy place for a nightcap or afternoon tea – they even have their own special blend.

CITY SLICKER
28 Establishment
2 5 Bridge Lane
Rooms from $330

The Merivale group run by the Hemmes family has plenty of experience running several of the CBD's most popular bars (which in Australia can often, confusingly, be called hotels) but, until the young siblings Justin and Bettina opened Establishment in August 2000, they had not tried their hand at a hotel. It was an ambitious project – the complete renovation and remodelling of the 19th-century George Patterson house, once a grand Sydney department store, which was gutted by fire in 1986. They have created not only the slickest of Sydney's contemporary design hotels but also a great restaurant est. (p. 131) and a fabulous lounge bar Hemmesphere (p. 152).

The hotel, accessed through a discrete entrance on Bridge Lane, is a study in modern sophisticated style. The 33 guest rooms and two split-level penthouse suites are decorated in either a soft, light or dark, edgy colour scheme. If you hanker for soothing calm ask for a room with pale carpeted floors, bleached American oak panelling, Italian straw-coloured cotton velour throws and jade and gold silk pillows. But if you are in a more dramatic mood, opt for the rooms with exposed timber warehouse ceilings, Japanese black timber floorboards, lilac suede daybeds and silver-grey chenille covered armchairs. All rooms come with sleek home entertainment and hi-fi systems and marble-clad bathrooms stocked with Bulgari toiletries. There's even a choice of bed pillows: feather and down or synthetic if you suffer from allergies.

Many of the building's original features have been retained, such as the soaring iron columns and pressed metal decorative ceilings most apparent in the main ground floor bar, one of the biggest and busiest in the city. More intimate and convivial is the Tank Stream Bar, adjacent to the hotel lobby and attracting the more discerning suits from the nearby stock exchange. Yet another bar, the Garden Bar and Asian Kitchen, occupies the lofty glazed atrium space in the middle of the building, and there's also Tank nightclub, one of the city's hippest dance spaces.

42 **Regents Court**
15 18 Springfield Avenue
Rooms from $190

One of Sydney's worst kept hotel secrets, Regents Court can be overlooked because of its location on a quiet cul-de-sac in the midst of King's Cross. The city's most raffish area, a hangout for drunks, prostitutes and addicts, will not appeal to everyone, but there's a bohemian charm to the Cross, and Regents Court is an ideal place from which to experience it.

Run by the MacMahon family since 1990, Regents Court is the kind of place where you may find many interesting characters, bon vivants and performance artists – all of whom come here to experience the hotel's unique hospitality and elegant design. Built as residential chambers in 1926, the hotel's 30 studio–style apartments were stylishly renovated by architect group D4 who created an impact through minimal fussiness and maximum use of classic designer furniture. Pieces by Josef Hoffman, Mies van der Rohe and Charles and Ray Eames will have you never wanting to leave the chocolate-brown and mushroom painted rooms – quite possible since they all have well-equipped kitchenettes and the hotel's obliging staff will go food shopping for you.

Even if self-catering isn't your thing, you may be tempted to use the barbecue on the splendid pebbled roof garden. This is the hotel's real treasure, an oasis of verdant shrubbery and fragrant flowers with outstanding views of the city.

COLOUR ME BEAUTIFUL

42 **Medusa**
22 267 Darlinghurst Road
Rooms from $270

Terry and Robert Schwamberg have been key figures in defining a distinct Sydney style of designer hotel with their Contemporary Hotels group. Since focusing their attention on luxury rental apartments, villas and beachhouses, such as Rockridge in Palm Beach (p. 185), the group's only hotel now is their beloved first, Medusa. This snakehaired temptress has been beguiling guests since 1998 with a fresh approach to the boutique hotel concept, banishing the monochrome and earth tones in favour of a bright palate of candy and funfair shades.

As outrageous as any Darlo drag queen, you won't fail to notice the babydoll-pink painted exterior of Medusa. Inside, award-winning designer Scott Weston has created a series of 18 rooms defined by bold furniture and even bolder colour schemes. Self-contained bathrooms have been cleverly built into the grand rooms at the front of the building where king-sized beds hover on raised wooden platforms. Plushly upholstered chaise longues tempt you to recline in the manner of a pop princess – think Kylie Minogue, one of the many celebrity guests to have sworn eternal devotion to Medusa.

If you're travelling with your beloved pooch, request a room beside the mauve painted courtyard with its soothing fountain and yellow lounge chairs – it will be spoilt with the best dog food and specially formulated dog shampoo.

ROCKSTAR PLAYGROUND

54 **Moog Hotel**
7 413 Bourke Street
Suite from $1,490

Paint it black. Perhaps Mick Jagger and fellow Stones gave Simon and Susanah Page, club promoters and founders of the Australian dance label Sublime, this advice for the frontage to their 'one-suite music hotel'. This Surry Hills terrace is the ultimate crash pad for rock gods or jet-setting DJs, a hotel fashioned as a playground for gadget- and style-obsessed adults.

Inspired by Philippe Starck's St Martin's Lane Hotel and other boutique boltholes they'd visited around the globe the Pages spent millions on this place. Every cent shows, from the red leather Edra Flap sofa to the gameboy-like remote control for the video and audio system and enormous boat-shaped Italian bath made from crushed almond shells in resin. Whimsical light fittings decorated with white feathers, crimson carpets and original artworks, including a multicoloured cube sculpture on the verandah, complete the unique look.

Even more opulent is the Pages's own apartment, also available to rent if your entourage is large. It has a couple of bedrooms, a piano, pool table, library, full kitchen and bronze-tiled bathroom that would be the envy of a Roman emperor. Elsewhere in the complex you can work out in a high-tech gym, record a CD in the state-of-the-art recording studio, then listen to the results through the underwater speakers in the courtyard plunge pool. Water cascading down the glass walls ensures privacy from any stray paparazzi in the adjoining public bar.

Behind the tigers eye-tiled bar is an extensive collection of premium quality spirits from which the staff can mix the secret concoction 'L'Amex Noir' – its recipe is only revealed when you buy one at a price that is equal to the number of the year. Rock stars may be tempted, as they may also be to hire the hotel's Jaguar XJR100 for the day. Lesser mortals, however, will have to content themselves with a seat on a translucent stool, a more reasonably priced cocktail from Moogbar's inventive list and the chance to absorb the whole Ab Fab, Alice-Cooper-in-Wonderland atmosphere of it all.

64 **The Chelsea**
1 49 Womerah Avenue
Rooms from $145

French provincial style meets inner-city contemporary chic at this 13-room boutique hotel on a quiet leafy street a few hundred metres from the café- and shop-lined streets of Darlinghurst and Paddington. Two 1870s terrace houses have been cleverly combined and restored, creating an elegant, unpretentious establishment surrounded by clipped hedges and potted trees.

The grey painted ironwork on the front verandah is picked up throughout the hotel in the scrolling steel legs of the hall table, a fabulous candelabrum in the living room and the basketweave chairs in the courtyard. There are also fresh cut flowers, gilt-edged mirrors and lush rugs thrown across tiled floors

The four small single rooms share bathrooms while the doubles have en suites with showers, and some have the original fireplaces and Louis XV–style chairs. The king suite has a private courtyard with palms and a water feature incorporating a shimmering wall of emerald and bronze tiles. An abstract work by Melbourne artist Katherine Bolum hangs above the bed and a metal ceiling fan, Italian Euroform chairs, sisal carpets and a marble-floored bathroom complete the blissful contemporary living effect.

The buffet breakfast is served in a serene courtyard that, without the box-planted lillypilly trees, could be in an exclusive European villa rather than on the cusp of the pumping heart of King's Cross. The friendly owners also run the Periwinkle Guesthouse in Manly – not in the same stylish class as the Chelsea but certainly one of the better accommodation options with individual character over on the North Shore.

THE FEMININE TOUCH

64 **Kathryn's on Queen**

18 20 Queen Street
Rooms from $180

An elegantly inscribed brass plaque marks this gem of a bed and breakfast in a National Trust listed building, dating from 1888, on the classiest street in Woollahra – perfectly situated for shopaholics who want to be close to some of the best spending opportunities in Sydney. The ebullient Kathryn Bruderlin runs an establishment that coasts along on plump cushions of calm, and ample doses of old European charm spiced up with carefree Australian wit.

The romantic décor with sunny splashes of Provence reflects Kathryn's whimsy. Beside the oak oval table and polished silver teapots in the comfortable lounge, you'll find bronze Chinese horses, chairs covered in a leopard-skin print and a fancy oriental plate picked up for 50 cents in a garage sale.

There are just three guestrooms, all doubles and only one en suite. The largest room, in the converted attic with a bathroom cleverly built into the old chimney, has a view across to the city with a glimpse of the Harbour Bridge. Downstairs, the front room has an 1860 French queensize bed and matching sidetable. Windows open on to a balcony with an original Sydney ironwork grill. Bathroom toiletries are from London's Molton Brown, and fine quality white towels and cotton sheets are embroidered with the B&B's copperplate script logo.

The house may be small but guests are given their privacy. The only time you'll see Kathryn beyond check-in and departure is when she's preparing her gourmet breakfasts: fresh and poached seasonal fruit, smoked salmon and eggs, plus all the best breads, cereals and preserves from nearby grocers Simon Johnson and jones the grocer (p. 70) are served on the hand-painted tile table in the courtyard. This is a delightful place to linger, surrounded by greenery, with the scent of jasmine and, if you crave more open space, Centennial Park is just across the road.

76 Ravesi's

9 118 Campbell Parade
Rooms from $195

Sydney's most famous beach has long been crying out for a decent designer hotel and with Ravesi's renovation, a Bondi landmark since 1914, it has finally got one. Its location couldn't be better with the surf breaking less than 200 metres away and all the shops and cafés of Campbell Parade, Gould and Hall Streets on its doorstep. It's the kind of place where a surfboard is more appropriate than a briefcase, although they happily accommodate guests with either.

The owners gave designer and artist Dayne van Bree free reign when he supervised the 2002 renovation of the hotel's 16 rooms, bar and restaurant. He ditched girly pastels in favour of a more hard-edged masculine approach. In the guestrooms the inspiration is an Aboriginal palate of colours: black, copper and bronze create a classic sophistication. Amenities are hidden to keep everything sleek and clean, a look carried through to the dazzling white bathrooms. Interest is added by Bree's abstract paintings in each room.

The penthouse has a plasma screen television and is decorated with a carving from Mali and woven baskets from Zimbabwe pinned to the wall. It opens out on to a glassed-in balcony, where you can lie back on a kidney-shaped canvas ottoman and play with a stone and fibre tick, tack, toe set.

The beachside location is reflected in the reception area's Indonesian shell studded light panels and the Gaudiesque whirlpool image sculpted in the restaurant's ceiling. At the lively ground floor bar concertina glass doors keep the light and sea breeze flooding in.

ANTIQUE STYLE

86 **Triketts**

2 270 Glebe Point Road
Rooms from $180

At the upmarket residential end of Glebe Point Road lies Triketts, a luxurious bed and breakfast in a lovingly restored Victorian mansion. Built by a wealthy merchant in 1880, it was taken over by the State government in 1923 to be a boys home and later the Children's Court. Liz Trickett, the genial proprietress, bought the building in the early 1990s and has nurtured it back to close to its former glory.

The charming antique character of Tricketts is established as soon as you cross the threshold: Victorian tessellated tiles line the hallway, ornate ceilings hang high above rare polished Kauri wood floorboards, warmed by Persian rugs. The building's highlight is the former ballroom – now the guest drawing room – with its gilded vaulted ceiling. A baby grand piano sits in the corner alongside leather Chesterfield sofas and a billiard table. Breakfast is served in the adjoining conservatory or, in summer, out on the secluded back deck overhung by bottle brush trees.

There are seven bedrooms, all with en-suite bathrooms and furnished with handsome pieces of heavy wooden furniture and exotic rugs. A mahogany four-poster bed in the honeymoon suite dates from 1825 and was brought to Australia by Admiral Harry McNicoll from India.

There are, however, some contemporary flourishes amid the antiquity: Liz commissioned a couple of striking Aboriginal paintings by Tony Sorbey that hang in the hallway, and the building is air-conditioned for summer and central heated for winter. The large verandahs and gardens at the front shaded by century-old trees are very peaceful – the ideal place to relax, read or plan your next foray into the city. There is guests' parking, and the Jubilee Park light rail stop is nearby giving you direct access to Darling Harbour and the CBD. Many of the attractions of the Inner West, including the Fish Markets and Glebe Point Road's Saturday markets (p. 88), are a short stroll away.

eat

Sydney is one of the world's great food cities, where the top chefs — Neil Perry, Tetsuya Wakuda, David Thompson, Christine Manfield — are superstars at home and abroad. While fluid in conception, modern-Australian fusion cuisine (mod-Oz in the local lingo) is what makes Australian chefs and their restaurants — which have a casual, laid-back atmosphere — such a revelation. It's about being bold with the flavour, colour and textures of food, but also about the subtleties of knowing when and how to combine ingredients and present them so they look as gorgeous as the décor or the dazzling view out the window.

14 **Quay**

20 Upper level, Overseas Passenger Terminal

When a restaurant has such an impressive location overlooking Circular Quay – Harbour Bridge to the left, Opera House to the right – what's on the plate has to be very attractive to make an impression. Fortunately Peter Gilmore is well up to the task, knowing how to create a 'wow' factor with his creations. Daring combinations, such as confit of belly pork with scallop or mud crab with tomato sorbet, may sound as outrageous as the psychedelic wave design of Quay's multicoloured carpet but somehow it all works perfectly. A Japanese influence is apparent in his layer cake of octopus, ginger slivers and the softest, freshest tuna sashimi dressed up with a patchwork of seaweed and tobiko. It's a dazzling dish, as beautifully presented as the tender, juicy squab with its breast meat forming a perfect heart. If you feel yourself falling, you'll know it's true love by the time the five textured Valrhona chocolate cake arrives – pure dessert bliss.

STAR PERFORMER

14 **Rockpool**

9 107 George Street

Neil Perry restaurants have come and gone but his multi-award-winning flagship Rockpool has endured. For over 15 years the quality and distinction of Perry's cooking has remained as bright as the single star that is the restaurant's logo and as madly glamourous as its décor, with its metallic blue carpet, mirrors and rose tapestry wall. A few key dishes – date tart, Chinese roast pigeon with prawn-stuffed aubergine – make regular appearances but otherwise the menu changes daily, reflecting the celebrity chef's devotion to using the freshest and finest produce. Reading the menu is an education: you'll learn how their shellfish are kept alive in four separate filtered tanks until they are needed; the provenance of key ingredients is meticulously noted; and the cheeses are described in loving detail. For the full experience of Perry's innovation, choose the eight course plus canapé and coffee tasting menu, which you can order with accompanying wines. It will be as precious and memorable as the 24-carat gold-leaf gilding on his lush chocolate cake.

ELEGANCE REVISITED

28 **Est.**

3 Establishment Hotel, 252 George Street

Recipient of *The Sydney Morning Herald* award for professional excellence in 2003, Peter Doyle is now running est. the flagship restaurant of the Establishment Hotel (p. 112). It is one of the most elegant dining rooms in the city, combining old colonial opulence with a contemporary design edge – an ornate pressed-lead ceiling is held aloft by twin ranks of Corinthian columns and chandeliers twinkle beside a metal cage wine store. The pewter grey upholstered chairs around the double-clothed tables are as comfortable as the easy going, professional service, taking the edge off what could so easily be – in other hands or in other cities – a too formal experience. Doyle uses the best of what is in season on his short but very appealing menus. Sample spice-crusted saddle of grain-fed venison or delicious grilled Hervey Bay scallops on an asparagus purée with morel mushrooms, but leave room for dessert. The passion-fruit soufflé with passion-fruit sorbet is divine, as is Doyle's tuile biscuit sandwich of musk melon ice cream topped with tequila and lime sorbet.

28

23

LIVING TREASURE
Tetsuya's
529 Kent Street

In his native Japan he would be a national treasure, in his adopted homeland Tetsuya (Tets) Wakuda is the only chef to have scored three chef's hats – the ultimate accolade in local food bible *The Good Food Guide* – for over a decade. His signature dish, a glowing orange pink confit of Petuna ocean trout, remains at the heart of his 12 or more course Japanese–French inspired degustation menu. Although many restaurants now serve something similar, no one can match Tets. His masterful technique is also evident in the deceptively simple floating island dessert, where separate shots of chocolate and berry sauce hide inside a fluffy white cloud of poached meringue. Like all great chefs, Tets knows that his fabulous food could easily be ruined if service is anything less than perfect so, as you admire the beautiful Japanese rock garden that is the restaurant's centrepiece, also marvel at his army of waiters who make you feel as special as the food. Book well ahead – royalty, Hollywood glitterati, and anyone interested in sublime food flock to this chic temple to gastronomy.

KING OF THAI

14 **Sailors Thai & Sailors Thai Canteen**
12 106 George Street

Part owner David Thompson may be concentrating on his award-winning London restaurant Naam but his grand design – the re-evaluation and glorification of Thai cuisine – remains the driving force at Sailors Thai and Sailors Thai Canteen. Thompson, author of the blockbuster *Thai Food*, learnt about the court cuisine of this southeast-Asian kingdom during the years he lived in Bangkok. The main restaurant, with a calming minimalist interior by Burley Katon Halliday, occupies the downstairs of the colonial sandstone Sailors' Home, and is a place for a memorable, lingering dinner, while the George Street level canteen, dominated by a zinc-covered communal table and open kitchen, is for casual dining. Both offer supremely tasty dishes that will shake up any green curry and fishcakes conceptions you may have of Thai cooking. The fruits of Thompson's knowledge translate into delicious morsels such as *ma hor*, a scintillating mix of palm sugar, minced prawns and chicken, deep-fried shallots, garlic and peanuts, or the *som dtam* salad of green papaya, salty pork and coconut rice.

NATIVE AUSTRALIAN

28 **Edna's Table**
16 204 Clarence Street

If you're looking for fine Australian cooking using native herbs, berries and meats such as wallaby, emu and crocodile, then Edna's Table is the place to come. Chef Raymond Kersh and his sister Jannice grew up in the outback and learnt much about the way Aboriginal people and early settlers used the fruits of this sunburnt land. This has been translated into a fusion cuisine that showcases the subtle flavours of lemon myrtle, pepperberry and native thyme in dishes that also reflect the influence of the Pacific rim. The six course native Australian degustation menu includes grilled kangaroo fillet with a warm beetroot and kumera salad and ponzu dressing, and crocodile and nori parcels in hot sour broth. The former 1850s ballroom has been utterly transformed with striking Aboriginal art, black velvet upholstered high-backed chairs and a black-and-white photo collage of the Kersh's lives. It's a personal touch that matches the friendly relaxed service.

42 **Otto**

3 8 The Wharf, 6 Cowper Wharf Road

In the midst of the esplanade running along the city side of Woolloomooloo's historic Finger Wharf sits the power princess of the lunch scene. Original owner Maurice Terzini may have decamped to Icebergs in Bondi (p. 140), but the formula of seriously good Italian food in a modern, sexy waterside setting still works a treat for the CBD's businessmen and women, ladies who lunch in designer sunglasses and haughty supermodels. They all know that Otto is still the place to see and be seen – as do the waiters, making, at times, an edgy, attitude-laden meal. Dinner tends to be more relaxed at this lovely spot for dusk-to-dark dining. They do traditional Italian well, with the best aged reggiano, plump olives and a melting beef carpaccio with truffle oil and parmigiano. The handmade pasta is delicious and al dente, and a whole grilled baby barramundi does justice to this great Australian fish.

 Salt

Kirketon Hotel, 229 Darlinghurst Road

Luke Mangan is Sydney's answer to Jamie Oliver, a larrikin Aussie bloke who makes a damn good sausage and whose local restaurants have been such a hit he's planning a new venture in New York. To get ahead of the Americans, hasten to Salt, the slickly designed restaurant that's part of Darlinghurst's boutique Kirketon Hotel where Mangan shares cooking duties with Mark Holmes. That's only to be expected since the ever busy chef now oversees Paddington's Bistro Lulu, and North Bondi's Moorish (p. 78)

as well as squeezing in restaurant consultancy and regular food articles for *The Sydney Morning Herald*. Salt offers innovative, risky mod-Oz food: roasted squab with pea purée and foie gras or a Szechuan–style duck breast with pickled pear showcase the chef's inspirations from around the world. A major bonus is their inventive vegetarian options such as eggplant and haloumi tart or tempura of goats' cheese stuffed zucchini flowers. A final tip: they also oversee the food at the Kirketon's hideaway bar Fix, including perhaps the best value and best tasting steak frites in the city.

54 **MG Garage**

8 490 Crown Street

Despite a partial change of owners and the removal of the sports cars that inspired the name, the vroom factor is still present at MG Garage. British chef Jeremy Strode has swept into town, trailing accolades from his stints at top Melbourne restaurants Langton's and Pomme, and causing Sydneysiders to acknowledge that there's culinary alchemy going on elsewhere in Australia. The traditional ingredients Strode uses, such as smoked eel, pigs' trotters and sweetbreads, are not often found on the menus of other top restaurants, and there are few other places in town that could be inventive enough to conjure five delicious dishes from a Dutton Park duck. Service remains exemplary and the dining room, even minus the sexy MG, still seduces with its smoky mirrors and wooden blinds. The two-course set lunch and pre-theatre deal (perfect if you're heading for the nearby Belvoir Street Theatre; p. 61) is an ideal way to sample this great restaurant at a fraction of the usual price.

NEW ASIAN GROOVE

 Longrain

3 85 Commonwealth Street

You'll probably have to wait a while for a place at the baronial communal table that dominates the restaurant in this chic Surry Hills warehouse conversion. It's no hardship though – head to the bar and have one of their famous bright green caipiroskas and settle onto a low stool while you wait your turn to sample chef Martin Boetz's contemporary, spicy southeast-Asian and Thai cuisine. As you would expect of a star alumnus of David Thompson's long gone and lamented Darley Street Thai, the food seldom fails to please, ranging from betel leaves topped with savoury morsels to jungle-curry tuna with wild ginger, apple and aubergine. They do great things with fish – some picked out of a tank and cooked to order. There's also a good range of vegetarian options and, rare for an Asian restaurant, a decent wine list. It can get noisy, but it's the buzz of people enjoying themselves and knowing that they're at one of the most happening spots in town.

64 Claude's

12 10 Oxford Street

Only 40 diners can eat at the intimate, austere Claude's, open five nights a week, making the waiting list long. Despite the exclusivity, it's worth signing up because of the exceptional modern French food of the man who is considered one of Australia's best chefs. Adelaide lad Tim Pak Poy has owned Claude's since the early 1990s. Named after the original owner, Claude Corne, this shoebox of a place, with walls decorated with antique limoge porcelain, is easily missed among the colourful boutiques of Oxford Street. It gained its reputation under the 1980s stewardship of Damien Pignolet (now running nearby Bistro Moncur) and his late wife Josephine. Corne's fruit soufflés are still on the menu, but in all other respects Poy has made this place and the light, inventive food his own. Depending on the season, savour Australian truffles, quail with watermelon, soft-shelled crab with mustard and lentils, sugared oysters with a tart, fruity tomato relish, or trout roe bound in smoked-salmon jelly and eaten with mother-of pearl-spoons.

MODERN FRENCH

64 Bistro Moncur

19 The Woollahra Hotel, 116 Queen Street

If there's one thing that the demanding citizens of Woollahra, one of Sydney's most upmarket neighbourhoods, know it's a decent place to eat. Damien Pignolet's Bistro Moncur has long been winning over these discerning customers with simple, well cooked food of the best quality. The jazzy black-and-white mural, wooden chairs and clothed tables lend it an air of Paris in the 1920s, but the feel remains very Sydney, particularly on a dazzlingly sunny day as you sip Chardonnay at one of their shaded verandah tables and tuck into their generous portions. You really can't go wrong with their sirloin steak and crisp shoestring chips or their fresh seafood, which could include a whole marron (a type of crayfish) from western Australia or the flavoursome spanner-crab omelette. Boudin noir and duck are house specialities. Some of Sydney's best chefs have passed through Pignolet's kitchens, including rising star Tim Pak Poy who now runs Claude's.

76 Sean's Panaroma
5 270 Campbell Parade

Sean Moran's casual restaurant at the north end of Bondi doesn't have the full panorama of the beach that the name hints at, but who needs that when they serve food this good? Whatever you order from the concise menu scribbled on small chalk boards above the service counter, it's guaranteed to be supremely tasty, easy on the eye and intriguing. Sean's reflects the laid-back style of the blue-eyed, youthful chef, but he's no slouch when it comes to choosing the best ingredients. His clam and prawn chowder is redolent of a great day by the ocean. Huge chunks of Flinders Island milk-fed lamb is medium-rare roasted with rosemary and served on a bed of minted mashed peas. The crisply deep fried blue-swimmer crab with aïoli cries out to be eaten with your fingers. During the day Moran's adjacent Aroma to Go café is a good place to drop by for a coffee, provisions for a picnic on the beach, or a sugar fix with Sean's chewy nougat.

PELICAN'S CHOICE
64 Catalina Rose Bay
29 1 Sunderland Avenue

A decade since its million-dollar makeover, Catalina remains one of the classiest harbourside operators. Perched on the brink of Rose Bay, next to the waterplane terminal (Australia's first international airport), and sporting sleek contemporary design and beautifully presented food, Catalina is the quintessential Sydney dining experience. Their cuisine is as seriously sexy as the curvaceous Alfred Humann-designed chairs. Flavours are bold: scarlet pomegranate seeds and amber onion jam on their entrée of raw Hiramasa Kingfish; a main of double-roasted duck is partnered with a luscious grilled fig and verdant dollop of chopped pistachios and lime. With such a soothing view this is a place to linger over dessert; the tasting platter might include a summer berry brulée tartlet, passion-fruit sorbet and sauterne jelly with cherries. No wonder that a pelican, nonchalantly perched on the polished concrete verandah, is eyeing your plate hungrily!

76 **Icebergs Dining Room & Bar**

17 1 Notts Avenue

Commandingly perched above an ocean-filled swimming pool and with an awe-inspiring view of the city's most famous beach, Icebergs certainly has the location, but it also has much more. The décor – a palate of cool aqua blues and silky candy pinks and mauves – chimes perfectly with the beachside environment. Wicker pod chairs dangle invitingly from the bar ceiling and lights flicker atop giant metal circle fixtures. Maurice Terzini and Andrea Mellas run the front of house with easy charm, marshalling a friendly group of waiters: men in black bow ties and deliberately rumpled white jackets, designed by Marcs, women in chic black. Last, but far from least, is Karen Martini's appealing modern Mediterranean cuisine. Both the Livornese–style fish stew with pearl pasta and bistecca alla Fiorentina, a slab of charcoal grilled sea-salt encrusted rib eye, are made to be shared – perfect for this romantic setting.

 64
Pier

27 594 New South Head Road

Australia has some of the world's best seafood and the ideal Sydney restaurant in which to sample it is Pier. The menu is a fisherman's tour of the continent: ocean trout from Tasmania, squid from the Hawkesbury, barramundi from the Northern Territory. Conscious of his restaurant's reputation, owner and chef Greg Doyle is prepared to go around the country to find what he wants, always insisting on the finest quality. It's always line caught, which is less stressful and damaging to the fish than it being netted. Try the moist-fleshed Murray cod, a freshwater species of the perch family, or the sweet tasting John Dory. Meaty scallops are perfectly matched with 'oysters' of chicken; pot-roasted lobster is spiced up with kaffir lime, peppercorns and Thai basil. With seafood this good you don't need much more, but Doyle offers very palatable desserts and has put together what he refers to as a 'kick-arse' wine list. The restaurant's location, jutting out into yacht-dotted Rose Bay, is a visual delight.

86 **Three Clicks West**

12 127 Booth Street

As house prices rise in the leafy inner-west suburb of Annandale, there has been a blossoming of classier places to eat run by ambitious chefs happy to push the boundaries of what to expect from a neighbourhood restaurant. Zenith on Booth Street, specializing in southern Italian cuisine, is good, but for sheer class and some sophisticated mod-Oz food that won't break the bank try Three Clicks West. Decorated in Art Déco–style, the split-level arrangement adds interest to the glowing, welcoming room. At these prices you really wouldn't expect an amuse bouche, but that's how a meal starts off and it only gets better. Roasted lamb sweetbreads and parsnips, smoked lamb cutlets with vol-au-vents or pan-fried monkfish with a corn velouté and a dusting of ground bacon are all delivered by waiters who shame other establishments with their friendliness.

BAYSIDE APHRODISIAC

86 **The Boathouse Blackwattle Bay**

3 End of Ferry Road

Situated in a converted boathouse with the fish market just across the bay beneath the sculptural expanse of the Anzac Bridge, you'd expect seafood to be a big deal, and it certainly is. This Glebe institution offers possibly the widest and tastiest selection of oysters in Sydney – on one night there may be nine varieties, ranging from the faintly metallic Nambucca River rock oyster to the saltier Smoky Bay Pacific oyster with its sweet finish. The salmon roe caviar with buckwheat blinis is another great entrée, while for a main course snapper pie with smoked tomatoes and mashed potato is a classic crusty champion expertly served at the table. Former Est. chef Martin Fleming has plenty of other great seafood dishes as well as interesting vegetarian and meat alternatives. The bar is at back of the shed, allowing all diners to enjoy the lively sparkle of city lights in the bay, and New Zealand artist Jenny Dolezel's quirky cartoon paintings are another talking point at this delightful restaurant.

BEACH-BLANKET BANQUET

96 Bathers' Pavilion Restaurant & Cafe

12 4 The Esplanade

In a city not short of restaurants with waterside views the Bathers' Pavilion Restaurant & Cafe in a glorious 1930s building fronting Balmoral Beach remains something special. From its open windows you look out on to the picturesque scene that made Balmoral Sydney's original bohemian artists' colony, which still inspires amateur painters today. There's much charm and whimsy in this designer beachshack's décor – colourful teatowel napkins, cutlery in whicker baskets, salt cellars by Dinosaur Designs – and it's carried through to the inventive Mediterranean-style food of chef Serge Dansereau. Scallop and oxtail ravioli, rabbit loin with sage gnocchi or roast squab in a foie gras sauce are some of the tempting delights. In the café, a blood orange, beetroot and radicchio salad goes down a treat, as does the rich sautéed duck liver with a vivid green pea purée. Whether you bring the kids and indulge in their delectable hot chocolate or get dressed up, hire a water taxi and zip over for a romantic degustation dinner, this is a restaurant where you will never feel out of place and will never want to leave.

drink

Breakfast in a convivial café, a nightcap in a chic bar – perfect bookends to the Sydney day. The city's drinking tastes tend to be Mediterranean influenced – coffee is more popular than tea, but ordering one requires learning the difference between a short black (espresso) and a flat white (espresso with hot milk). No study is required to appreciate the pick of Sydney's watering holes, which range from glorious Art-Déco and heritage-listed pubs to bars setting international standards in interior design and cocktail creation.

42 **bills**

24 433 Liverpool Street

Every neighbourhood should be lucky enough to have a bills. Bill Granger, legend of Sydney's breakfast and lunch scene and prolific cookbook writer, has two eponymous cafés in the Darlinghurst–Surry Hills style nexus. This sunny Darlinghurst corner terrace is where it began in 1993. With its huge shared blonde wood table, laden with the daily papers and the best style and food magazines, this is the epitome of a laid-back café in which to while away a morning or afternoon. The menu, chalked up on a huge blackboard, doesn't change much, but there's no reason to when it has some of Sydney's best breakfast dishes including creamy scrambled eggs, which *The New York Times* calls the best in the world. The ricotta hotcakes with fresh banana and honeycomb butter are pure bliss on a plate. For an ideal brunch order the dazzling sweetcorn fritters with roast tomato, spinach and bacon. The staff are unfailingly wonderful, dispensing Grinders coffee with alacrity, and giving you the space to enjoy the whole communal experience.

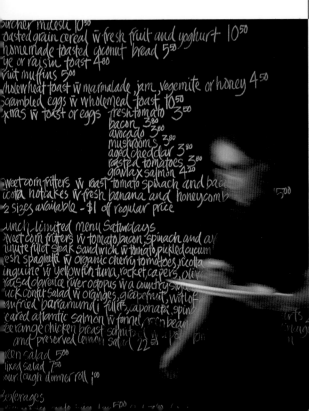

54 **Danks Street Depot**

20 2 Danks Street

If you want a peek at one of the inner city's hottest development zones visit Waterloo where warehouses are being turned into sleek modern apartments and shops. The starting point for this gentrification is 2 Danks Street, a collection of nine galleries and the über-stylish café and bistro Danks Street Depot, all occupying a former bus depot. At a long communal table enjoy a tasty and crispy corned-beef-rueben sandwich with sauerkraut or their sinful bread-and-butter pudding studded with melted chocolate buttons and ripples of homemade jam. If you like the jam you can buy a pot to take home. One of the attached art spaces is Brenda May Gallery, specializing in emerging Australian artists working in a variety of mediums. The sculptures and three-dimensional works are great, and there's also a collection of jewelry and ceramics, some from southeast Asia. Also worth a look are the Still Gallery, focusing on contemporary photography and photo-based art, and a branch of the successful Auckland-based Gow Langsford Gallery.

76 Brown Sugar
3 100 Brighton Boulevard

Bags of hippy, not hip, charm, cheerful, attitude-free waiters, a wholesome and appealing menu and zingingly perky coffee with froth so thick you could stand a spoon up in it – what's not to like about this rustic north Bondi café? A multicoloured mosaic of jars are stacked by the door, homemade jams and sauces are displayed above the cash till and a Buddha statue sits on the kitchen shelf. The signature dish is 'black-stone eggs' – poached eggs, bacon, oven-roasted tomatoes and cheese on an English muffin, but you could go for the sweeter route of pancakes with fresh fruit and yoghurt or opt for a colourful house salad. Take the papers for a lazy weekend brunch and some extra cash to go shopping at Remo (p. 165) next door.

SEASIDE SOPHISTICATE
96 Manly Wharf Hotel
15 Manly Wharf, East Esplanade

Manly's claim to be 'a thousand miles from care' could just as easily be applied to the Manly Wharf Hotel at the north edge of the redeveloped shopping centre that greets you as you step off the ferry from Circular Quay. With a bar this good looking and perfectly located, you'd be excused for not going any further on your explorations of Manly. Split into four areas – waterside restaurant, jetty bar, large public bar and more intimate lounge bar – the hotel has the most stylish décor on this side of the harbour. Bamboo pole screens, smooth pebbles set in the walls, funky vinyl barrel stools on a wavy red carpet and aqua blue mosaic tiles as cool as the dappled harbour waters: it's a look that's both sophisticated and casually chic. There's the usual range of cocktails and some very palatable dishes at the restaurant. Order another dozen oysters and glass of Chardonnay and let the ferries come and go as you cast your cares away.

BLARNEY CHARMER
86 **The Welcome Hotel**
13 91 Evans Street

The twinkling Irish charm of the Welcome Hotel is summed up in the legend of Winston, the stowaway dog that is this gastro-pub's mascot – read this fanciful tale on the wall of the beam-and-brick traditional Irish pub that's been around since 1877. Dark timber tables, chunky chairs and the obligatory antique Guinness adverts lend the requisite old-fashioned ambience to the main bar area where you can tuck into the well-crafted, elegantly simple cuisine of Irish chef Fiona Healy. A beef and Murphy's Irish stout pie goes down very nicely with one of their hand pulled ales. As well as Guinness, there's also Kilkenny and Old Speckled Hen on tap. The traditional beer-battered fish is accompanied by that rarest of foods in a Sydney restaurant: hand-cut chips. When, like all good Irish bars, the Welcome gets loud and smokey in the evening, escape to the beer garden or smart patio restaurant space.

THERE SHE SAILS
14 **Palisade**
2 35 Bettington Street

A sense of history pervades the Palisade, a First World War-era pub berthed like some magnificent ocean liner on a corner in the Rocks. Generations of dock workers and sailors have supped here, enjoying the warm conviviality, the breeze from the harbour and the cold, freshly pulled ale. With the redevelopment of Walsh Bay the docks are all but gone, but customers still come to appreciate this heritage, the lack of pounding music and the highly respected restaurant in its butterscotch painted first-floor dining room. Bankers, brokers and politicians are regular patrons of elegant dishes such as Martini-cured salmon with slivers of fennel or veal and spiced beetroot. Should you wish to stay, there are some simply furnished guestrooms on the upper stories.

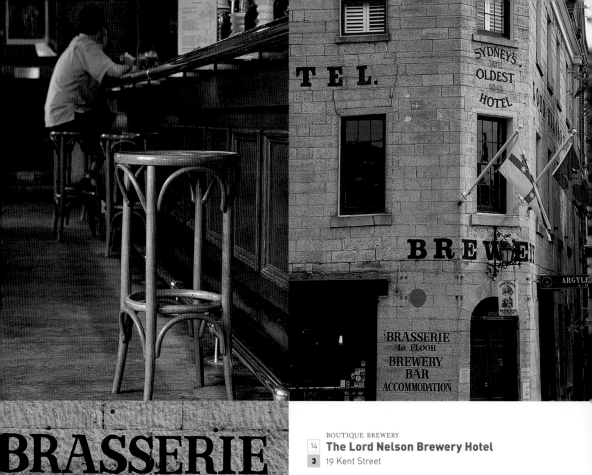

BOUTIQUE BREWERY

14 The Lord Nelson Brewery Hotel

3 19 Kent Street

There are a lot of pubs in the Rocks that trade on their heritage value but few that have the true credentials of the Lord Nelson. Ale has been served in the handsome sandstone house on the corner of the very English style Argyle Place since 1831, although the hotel only got its current name in 1841, just over 35 years after Nelson's defeat at Trafalgar. Read all about it in the framed 1805 edition of *The Times* on the bar wall and also inspect the pub's original licence. The Lord Nelson is particularly notable as one of Sydney's very few micro-breweries. They brew six types of beer on site, including the dark, chocolatey Old Admiral, bronze-coloured and more caramel-flavoured Victory Bitter, and the light golden Aussie–style Trafalgar Pale Ale. There's even a wheat beer named in honour of former US Vice President Dan Quayle who dropped by in 1989. Upstairs is the formal Nelson's Brasserie with a portrait of old Horatio above the fireplace. Try their signature dish of smoked fish pie or Goan–style lamb shanks.

Lotus

22 Challis Avenue

Your lounge at home is probably bigger than this tiny space, but it is unlikely to be as sexily decorated, as full of beautiful people and as blessed with a genial barman whose skills are rated among the best in Australia. Hidden like a prohibition bar behind the buzzy Lotus restaurant is a cosy, smoke-free, jewel box. One wall is plastered with Florence Broadhurst gold and silver palm-print wallpaper, another with moulded snakeskin. Box stools upholstered in lotus-patterned brocade nestle beside mirrored tables. Behind the onyx bar, award-winning cocktail maestro Marco Faraone turns on his Italian charm making everyone feel welcome. His 50 concoctions are inventive: there's the Rat Pack of Martinis, one each dedicated to Frank, Dino, Sammy, Lawford and Bishop, and the list of classic mixes gives you the history behind each one, such as the Margarita (born at a party thrown by Margarita Soamas for hotelier Nicky Hilton in 1948 in Acapulco, apparently).

CENTRAL-AMERICAN JOE

96 **Don Adán Coffee House**

8 5 Spit Road, shop 2

The coffee at Don Adán comes from Marcala, a town in the mountains of Honduras, where the Barios family have been growing it for over 140 years. The high altitude of the plantations results in a fuller flavoured coffee but with less caffeine. It's imported into Sydney as raw green beans and roasted on a weekly basis to give customers the most flavourful coffee they can sample this side of the harbour. An added bonus is that you can enjoy your cup in a funky, laid-back atmosphere with a painted Marc Chagall–style ceiling and a gallery of works by local artists, while snacking on a bagel sandwich or stack of pikelets. It's also nice to know that ten cents from every coffee sold goes to help maintain a UNICEF library in Honduras.

Built in 1940 the heritage-listed Civic is one of Sydney's grandest Art Déco–style pubs. It was a key performance venue with bands such as INXS and Midnight Oil raising the roof here in the late 1970s, but the following decade was less kind and at one point it closed as its future depended on the development difficulties that afflicted the adjacent World Square complex. Reborn in the late 1990s it is again one of the CBD's best drinking and entertainment venues, offering something for most tastes on its three levels. The ground-floor salon bar, with heavy red velvet drapes and original Déco tiling, is where the original spirit of the Civic is best experienced with DJs keeping the patrons happy and dancing at weekends. Upstairs is the Déco brasserie, a laid-back dining room and cocktail bar with a jazz theme, while in the basement the renovated theatre, with its profusion of mirror balls, is an intimate cabaret and performance space. Check their schedules to catch stellar Sydney artists such as Deni Hines, Tom Burlinson and the fantastic Paul Capsis.

Guillaume at Bennelong Bar

22 Sydney Opera House

The Opera House's premier bar and restaurant is the best location in which to appreciate the interior majesty and technical accomplishment of Jørn Utzon's architectural masterpiece. The concrete ribs of the building, holding up the tiled, sail-like roof, are exposed like the skeleton of a great whale. For pre- or post-concert drinks and delicious nibbles from the tapas menu of expat French chef Guillaume Brahimi, this is the place to be, preferably with a glass of sparkling wine or a house cocktail, perhaps a Madame Butterfly – vodka and Pimms muddled with lychees. The low slung chocolatey suede-upholstered swan seats and mossy green carpet add a luxurious touch, while the decorative gaggle of contemporary *larrakitj* (Aboriginal burial poles) are a poignant reminder that this land once belonged to the Aborigine Bennelong and his kin.

28 **Hemmesphere**

4 Establishment Hotel, 252 George Street

With a luxurious mix of silky fabrics and earthy tribal style, gauze curtains hanging from exposed rafters past padded silk walls in citrus colours to a custom-made striped carpet of reds, golds and browns, Hemmesphere can't fail to seduce. Melbourne-based interior designers Hecker Phelan worked with the Hemmes siblings to create the Establishment Hotel's private lounge bar (see p. 112). Cocoon yourself in a mass of silk cushions, perch on an ottoman fit for a sultan and rest your drink on a carved plinth. The bar's wickedly potent absinthe-based cocktails and slinky lounge music (available on a house CD) eases you into ultra exclusive mood. At the back of the vast room, beyond a beautiful wooden panel, the super stylish Japanese food bar, Sushi-e, rests on an island of pristine Italian marble and glowingly lit copper. The zen like simplicity of the food, including tasting spoons filled with deep fried oysters, seared tuna, snapper sashimi and char-grilled octopus, throws into sharp relief the mad opulence of it all.

Lounging on one of the giant ottomans in the Water Bar, gazing up at the enormous goods conveyors and soaring criss-cross of beams spanning the cathedral-like space, is likely to make you feel pretty small in the scale of things. Time for another cocktail from the purple glowing slate bar and surrounded by oversized angle-poise lamps. The grand design of this award-winning bar makes perfect sense out of a space where bails of wool and other cargo began their voyage around the world. Dating from 1910 the Woolloomooloo Finger Wharf (so called because it sticks out like a finger into the harbour) is the largest timber pile wharf in the world. Handsomely restored and remodelled during the 1990s it has become an urban oasis of apartments, restaurants, cafés and the W Hotel, the first outside of North America. During the wharf's heyday many a soldier, immigrant and tourist embarked or disembarked here; now the good times are back, and the Water Bar is certainly the place to celebrate.

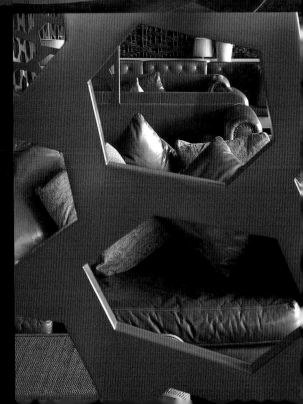

Occupying pole position on the King Street Wharf development, Loft is built for Sydney's gilded youth. The space is as large and muscular as any Bondi surfer, decked out predominantly in tanned leather sofas and chairs and divided by geometric cut-out screens in burnt orange. Designer Dale Jones-Evans has softened the effect with the butterscotch floral fretwork on the ceilings and walls, a flapper-girl tangerine swirl of beaded lightshades over the bar and a scattering of paisley print cushions. With the warm evening light bouncing off Darling Harbour, enjoy tapas, oysters and cocktails taking their inspiration from the Mediterranean, Middle East and Far East. Sip a Baghdad iced tea and keep your eyes peeled for royalty: Prince Harry was a regular here during the 2003 Rugby World Cup.

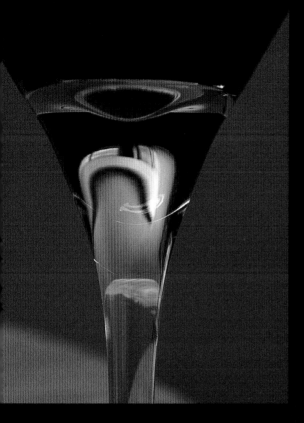

54 Middle Bar
5 383 Bourke Street, Taylor Square

On the first floor of Kinsela's, an old boozer on Taylor Square, is the altogether more stylish Middle Bar. Its spacious glassed-in balcony is a prime place to watch the flashy, trashy party guys and girls of this louche part of town drifting below. Order one of their signature stick drinks, fruity Caiprioskas or a spiced rum and Pimms Spice Island cocktail to toast Taylor Square's neat bricked-in island of grass and fountains, which not long ago had only scrappy palms, causing the locals to dub it fondly Gilligan's Island after the 1960s US TV show. Get comfy inside as you slip down into the soft cushions of the sunken, Hugh Hefner–style seating area while the DJ spins another number. It's a bar for the metrosexual generation.

GAY ABANDON
42 The Tilbury Hotel
6 12–18 Nicholson Street

There's been a pub on this spot in Woolloomooloo for about 150 years, although the present building dates from 1945. In December 2002 the Tilbury reopened its doors following an ambitious, yet sensitive makeover by designers Farnham and Finlay. The warmth of the original coffee and mustard tiling has been picked up in the chocolate-and-tan coloured leather upholstery of the bar and restaurant seating and the grainy cherrywood chairs. The beer garden has a Balinese feel with raw timber recliners shaded by a beautiful frangipani tree, triangle pillows and a black tiled water feature backed by a stand of lush bamboo. Lit by teardrop shaped red storm lamps this is a place for kicking back in the evening and listening to the DJs who take to the decks five nights a week. The restaurant's menu of modern Italian cuisine changes daily and there's a great wine list that includes everything from crisp, inexpensive Chardonnay to $500 vintage bottles of Penfolds Grange.

42 **Chicane**

28 1A Burton Street

Tucked away off a pretty square, known as the 'Paris' end of Burton Street, is Chicane, a darkly sophisticated modern Australian bar and restaurant, styled for all seasons. For sultry nights there's a terrace area shaded by potted foliage. On chillier days (Sydney does get them) there are two roaring open fires, ideal for curling up in front of the flames on winter nights and enjoying the seductive softness of a room burnished with rustic reds, earthy browns and mustardy ochres. It's a very seductive and convivial setting in which to sample a drop from their extensive wine list or one of their elegantly conceived classic and new cocktails – Tom Collins comes in five fruity variations. Cocktails can be made either with local bubbly or real champagne, and there's a grazing menu of fine bar snacks available until the small hours. The polished concrete island bar divides the club-like bar space with its high-backed armchairs from the retro feeling dining room with intimate leather lined booths,which serves chef Nathan Tillott's meaty menu.

NEW ASIAN DREAM

42 **jimmy liks**

8 186–88 Victoria Street

Named after a character in a Ruth Park novel, jimmy liks pulls off that tricky double act of being stylishly minimalist yet warmly inviting – perhaps because of the alluring light glowing behind the American oak battens along the wall that divides the bar from the restaurant and the candles flickering on the tables. British chef Will Meyrick sought inspiration from his southeast-Asian travels to create the casual dining menu. This is Thai street food for inner-city sophisticates, as tastily seductive as the elongated gauze Chinese lantern hanging above the communal jarrah wood table. With an enticing list of Asian-inspired mixed drinks, such as the signature Kyoto Protocol cocktail – cucumber and kiwifruit muddled and shaken with white rum, sake and apple liqueur – it's guaranteed to be a long sultry night at this hip Potts Point joint.

RETURN OF THE RAJ

42 **The Victoria Room**
23 235 Victoria Street, level 1

From the blazing sunlight of modern Darlinghurst stumble up the oddly uneven stairs into the seductive, half light of this homage to the Indian Raj. Madly whirling ceiling fans send ripples through the cane curtains dividing the tapas–style dining area from the long, backlit bar. The huge space is furnished with a jumble of Chesterfield sofas, Louis XV–style chairs, low marble-topped tables, leafy potted palms and a baby grand piano. At weekends they open at 4 pm and serve high tea with dainty crustless smoked salmon sandwiches, pukka mini pork pies and scrumptious tiny chocolate and raspberry cakes. As night falls the too-cool-for-school crowd arrive to revel in this very un-Sydney like experience, steadying their nerves at the downright decadence of it with a ginger and lemongrass Martini or the vodka-based raspberry debonair. It's as if the colonial days were never over.

shop

Sydneysiders seldom miss an opportunity to go on a spending spree, whether at the weekend markets in Paddington and Bondi for the newest fashion or jewelry designs or scouring chic boutiques in Double Bay for homewares to decorate the apartment of their dreams. Women's fashion covers everything from super sexy swimwear to dreamy ball gowns. Men are better served at the casual end of the fashion spectrum — think surfer chic or streetwear with an urban edge. Some of the recommendations below you will know, others will make you wonder why it took you so long to make a shopping trip down under.

ROMANCING THE CLOTHES

64 **Collette Dinnigan**

8 33 William Street

New Zealand-born designer Collette Dinnigan's madly romantic and feminine Wild Hearts range of luxurious lingerie, produced by UK department store Marks & Spencer, is displayed alongside her full collection at her flagship William Street boutique. Decorated like Marie Antoinette's closet, with grand peppermint satin drapes fringed with cream tassles, a vine-covered courtyard with a giant metal birdcage in the corner, and rose-design filigree staircase, this is the prettiest setting for Dinnigan's distinctive brand of old-style, high-glamour clothing. The attention to detail and use of fine and exclusively made fabrics on her classic slip dresses and evening gowns is what makes them special. Satin and silk are trimmed with guipure lace, some woven through with shimmering metallic threads. Her beautifully hand-beaded silk georgette dresses are adored by movie stars who regularly turn to Dinnigan for a frothily glamourous gown when the red carpet beckons.

Justine Pratten's sassy range of candy coloured handmade sandals and pumps, accessorized with matching wallets, bags, purses and belts, has graduated from a Paddington Market stall to a cute terrace berth on William Street. The shoe styles range from stilettos for cocktail parties to flip-flops that are perfect for the beach. A great match for designer jeans are the unique range of court shoes with a cute kitten heel covered with vintage American T-shirts. Each pair is a one-off: key designs from the printed cotton T-shirts are cut out and applied to calf leather.

Justine's sister Monique makes the fine, fun beaded jewelry on sale, and they have recently started to sell the clothing range of Nocturne from Paris – some of these silk garments are detailed with the same Swarovski crystals that lend a sparkling touch to Justine's footwear.

The Welsh-born immigrant who established Australia's oldest department store had a mission: 'to sell the best and most exclusive goods'. Since 1838 David Jones has stuck to that goal, making it a successful institution across Australia. The flagship branch spans Elizabeth and Castlereagh Streets and, when it opened in 1927, it single-handedly shifted the commercial heart of the city downtown from Martin Place to beside Hyde Park. On the seventh floor of this handsome building is the great restaurant where HRH Queen Elizabeth II attended a State banquet in 1954. In the store where Australia first saw Dior's New Look, today's fashionistas can find the very best Australian designers from the desirable denims of Sass & Bide to the fabulous finery of Akira Isogawa (p. 169) and Collette Dinnigan. Their scrumptious food hall is in the basement of the attached Market Street store – a major renovation has left it looking fabulous. Stop by for champagne and freshly shucked oysters at their oyster bar or stock up for a gourmet picnic in Hyde Park.

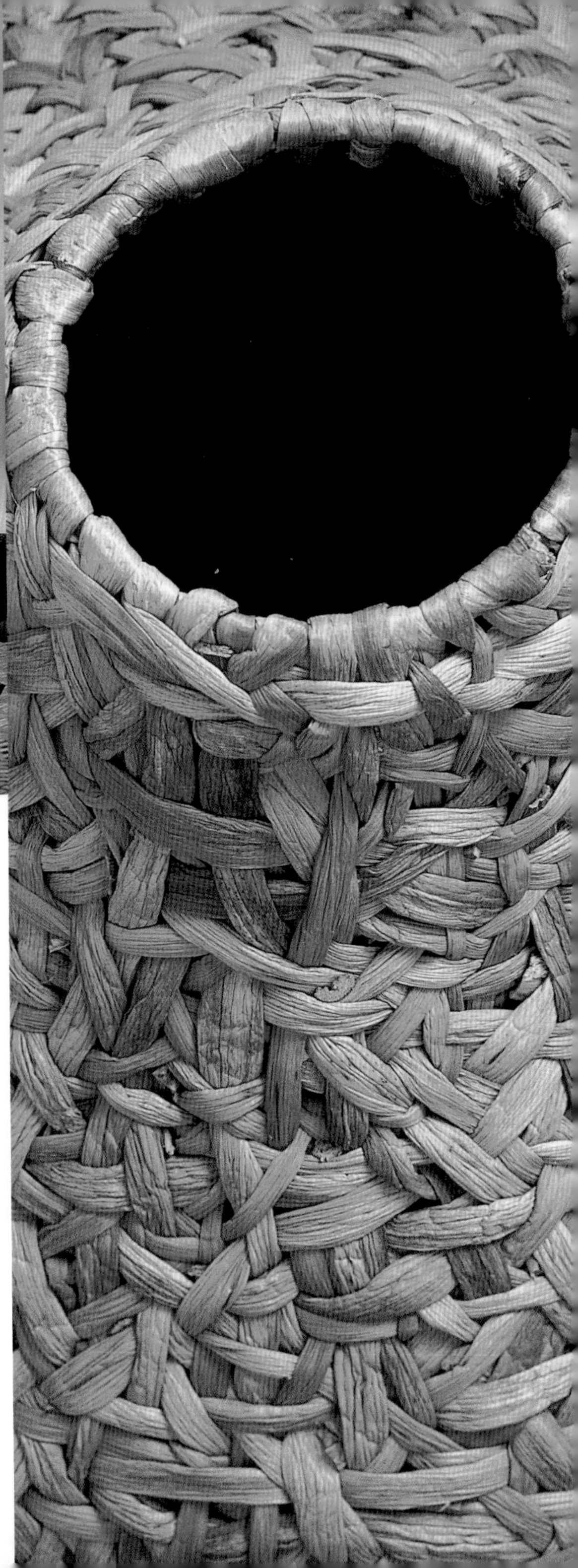

RAW BEAUTY

64 **Papaya**

24 15 Transvaal Avenue

Karen Lang and Robyn Connelly began the Papaya brand of tactile, sensual and sophisticated homewares in 1996. Amidst changing fashions they have stuck to their vision of sourcing and commissioning goods made from natural materials that have a clean design and simplicity of line and form. Their wide range of baskets, trays and boxes woven from water hyacinth offer a new approach to storage. Enhance the mood at home or in the garden with their luminous votive candle holders, lanterns and hurricane lamps in glass, taffeta and resin, and even the home office can be given a makeover with their fabric-covered office storage boxes and files. These savvy Double Bay purveyors of laid-back taste have their globally trained eye on craftmanship, sourcing top quality glass from Eastern Europe and stocking established Australian brands such as Helen Kaminski's natural fibre hats.

Andrew McDonald

9 58 William Street

The atelier and showroom of Andrew McDonald, bootmaker to Princess Amadala and Anakin Skywalker of *Star Wars* fame, can be found on William Street. The movie makers from nearby Fox Studios come here when they need the best footwear for their stars. Shoes are made for both sexes, but McDonald's traditional men's range is most eye-catching. Beside piles of old *National Geographic* magazines and nick-nacks in a battered wooden printer's tray you'll find brogues, slip-ons, and ghillies (the lace-up shoes traditionally worn with a kilt) in conservative yet subtly subversive styles. The shape may be more pointed than usual and detailing, such as spiral stitching or cross-hatch scoring of the leather, adds another level of interest to shoes. He takes his inspiration from Lobbs in London where he learnt his trade before heading back to Sydney and opening his own store. He can make any style in any leather and, because his shoes are all bespoke, they will fit perfectly.

MUST HAVE SWIMWEAR

Zimmermann

13 24 Oxford Street

You're going to be spending a fair amount of time at the beach in a swimsuit while you're in Sydney and you'll want to look good, so there's really only one place to go. Designer Nicky Zimmermann, high priestess of Australian swimwear, and her sister and business partner Simone are the driving forces behind the eponymous label. Their rise from a store on South Dowling Street in the early 1990s to the dizzy heights of the world's top department stores, including Saks, Barneys and Selfridges, has been inexorable. Like Collette Dinnigan they have gone into partnership with the UK's Marks & Spencer to develop swimwear for an international market. Their Paddington stores showcase the best of their fashion swimwear made from stretchy, high-gloss jersey that is always supremely well cut. Snap up one of Zimmermann's range of slinky slip dresses and tops to complete the Australian beach-babe look.

96 **Spacejunk**

17 30 Pittwater Road

Gina O'Neill is passionate about fashion, her husband
Marcie is equally mad about art. They've combined their
interests in Spacejunk, a showcase for Antipodean
creativity. The Manly shop, named after a line in a song
Marcie wrote for Gina, acts as a gallery for local artists, with
exhibitions changing every three weeks, and a fashion
nexus for both sexes. Oska Wright, artist and co-creator of
the local streetwear label tsubi, has exhibited his paintings
alongside tsubi's distressed, stylishly cut jeans and punk
T-shirts. Among the carefully chosen range of emerging
and established edgy, young fashion designers you'll find
the practically undefinable Zambesi, a womenswear brand
known for layered clothing and unusual fabrics and design.
The dark, gothic look is present in the clothes of Nom*D
and young Australian designer of the year Claude Maus –
his shirts and knitwear have the quality of Italian tailoring.
They also stock natural toiletries by New Zealand's Living
Nature, hand-painted silk dolls by Saffron Craig and – if
you're inspired to create your own art – Lomo cameras.

Remo Giuffré is the man who put a funky fez, Cole Porter lyrics and the word 'Eternity' on Sydneysiders's T-shirts, super strong Yorkshire Gold tea in their mugs and Kiehl's toiletries in their bathrooms. His mini department store (on the corner of Oxford Street and Crown Street) closed in 1997 but, following a stint in the US, Remo has returned online and at this 'cellar door' operation in north Bondi. You can choose from scores of distinctive prints on generously cut black or white heavyweight cotton T-shirts. The elegant copperplate 'Eternity', as chalked by Arthur Stace across Sydney for 37 years from 1930, is a cult print as are the maps of Australia overwritten with the word 'Home'. The Remo concept, though, is more than a collection of iconic, quirky and clever T-shirts – Giuffré has travelled the world seeking out quality items imbued with the passion of their makers. His eclectic range includes classic 1950s New Zealand-made toys, fine Valobra soap from Italy, 'curiously strong' Altoids peppermints from Wales and the Acme Thunder, the official whistle of the London bobby.

Generations of Sydney men have gone to Gowings for their work and leisure wear and to have their hair trimmed at the cheap barber shop. Indeed 'Gone to Gowings' is a phrase that has passed into the Australian language as a synonym for going broke, facing a calamity or suffering a hangover – somewhat unfair given that Gowings has been successfully in business for over 135 years. At all their stores, the flagship of which you'll find on the corner of George and Market Streets, you can stock up on the very best Australian clothing and footwear. From Bludstone utility boots through R. M. Williams's moleskin trousers and Bonds singlets (vests in the American vernacular) to Akubra bushwacker hats, you can kit yourself out from head to toe in Gowings. It's a great place for hunting out odd presents and nick-nacks – everything from voodoo dolls and bongo drums to handstitched leather coin purses, scooters and globes.

CULTURAL SURFER
64 Mambo
2 17 Oxford Street

Founded by Dare Jennings in 1984, Mambo's aim was to create a range of clothing that embraced art, politics, music and humour, and that looked great if you were into surfing. Whacky, irreverent and wildly colourful cartoon designs, such as a dog farting musical notes and Australia's emblematic emu and kangaroo transmuted into boozy archetypes poised beside a giant beercan, define what Mambo does best. You can rely on them for boardshorts and over-sized T-shirts in eye-poppingly bright colours and designs. In 2000 they designed the Australian team's uniform for the Sydney Olympics, and recently the Mambo look has widened to embrace all manner of casual clothing with more edgey contemporary designs. Still it's the larrikin artwork of masters such as Reg Mombassa and Rockin' Jelly Bean that makes a visit to Mambo's original Oxford Street store or their outlets in the Rocks or Bondi, a pilgrimage to the font of popular Australian fashion culture.

THE LOOK OF THE LAND
76 Cloth
18 207 Clovelly Road

There are echoes of Lucienne Day and William Morris in the contemporary printed fabrics of Julie Patterson and yet they are also distinctly Australian. The British textile designer settled in Australia in 1989 and has been drawing on her experience of the land ever since. Her designs often start as sketches of the countryside seen from the air as she flies to her commercial printer. She then makes paintings (some on display in the shop window) and plays around with the designs on the print table that dominates the showroom, surrounded by rolls of hemp that reflect the earthy tones of Australia. This is furnishing fabric, but Patterson's prints can also be applied to cottons and silks for clothing; she's collaborated with Akira Isogawa and Collette Dinnigan. Nothing is wasted, she uses off cuts for patchwork cushions, lampshades, bags and a charming series of cloth dolls with distinct personalities: Isabella the school captain, Ezra the bookworm or the rock chick. The fabrics are exported to New Zealand and Japan and she also plans to take on London and New York.

SHARP STREETWEAR
64 **Morrissey**
6 372 Oxford Street

When Qantas needed new designs for their flight attendants' uniforms they called Peter Morrissey, the man considered the Tom Ford of Australian fashion. Gold Coast meets Miami Vice is the look and feel of his laid-back yet glamourous streetwear and more formal fashion for both sexes – part of a casual chic movement in Australian fashion that encompasses brands such as Saba, Calibre and Wayne Cooper (pages 66, 38 and 33 respectively). His boutiques, found on the Paddington section of Oxford Street and at Sydney Central Plaza on George Street, cover everything from a stylish pair of jeans, monogramed with his trade mark 'M', to a sexy cocktail dress or sharp suit. The mirrored walls, sleek lines and metallic finishes of his shops set the tone for the hard-edged style of clothes and accessories, which includes sunglasses, jewelry and leather goods.

54 **Wheels & Doll Baby**

4 259 Crown Street

If you've always wanted to be a rock goddess or the pampered playmate of a zillionnaire, sashay down to the Wheels & Doll Baby's flagship boudoir in Surry Hills to get yourself the kind of outfit that goes with clutching a triple platinum disk or wearing a diamond the size of a boiled egg. The leopard print carpet, velvet drapes and French panelling of the boutique make the perfect setting for designer Melanie Greensmith's fabulous silky, frilly or polka-dotted outfits, guaranteed to get you noticed. Shocking pink, devilish black, lascivious lace, fake fox-fur trim and dazzling diamante-studded collars and bows are the key notes, loved by Hollywood sex kittens and global pop icons. The list of devotees of Greensmith's punky, baby-doll slips, t-shirts and leather jackets reads like a who's who of *Rolling Stone*. It's trashy glamour for the girl (and occasional guy) most likely to go places.

 96 **Glamourpuss**

16 58 Darley Road

The magic of 1950s Hollywood is the inspiration for Samantha Tunbridge's Glamourpuss range of purses, handbags, vanity cases, luggage and wallets, available from her Manly store and online. If you want to look like Grace Kelly as you glide through the airport lounges of the world, then tote one of Tunbridge's cherry red or midnight black Maggie the Cat beauty cases. The faux-alligator skin will fool everyone with its authentic texture and sheen, as will the divinely sensual faux-leopard fur. The Vintage Glamourpuss range of shoulder bags, each named after classic movies, are unique: Tunbridge travels to the US three times a year to source fabulous mid-20th-century printed cotton called Barkcloth, which comes in lush floral and abstract designs in vivid technicolours. The sizes given to the shop's Starlet and St Tropez range of silky satin dresses are whimsically named – ranging from a petite Audrey (Hepburn) to the full-figured Jayne (Mansfield).

 BEYOND FASHION
64 **Akira Isogawa**

16 12a Queen Street

Like Tetsuya Wakuda (p. 132), the other famous Sydney-based Japanese expat, Akira Isogawa has imaginatively adapted his native culture into a new, hybrid form that is outside current trends and yet trendsetting in itself. Akira's beautiful, ethereal clothes embrace the decorative traditions of Japan, but also reflect the artistic freedom and functionality of his adopted homeland. The best of these clothes are on view at his Woollahra boutique where there are dresses made from screen-printed fabrics of his own design and gowns with delicate hand finishing. Pieces of silk kimono material provide details on waistbands or straps, and embroidery, suede and leather are used inventively. The teddy-bear backpack combined with bodice was inspired by the Japanese trend-watching magazine *Fruits*. In 2002, the Object Gallery (p. 170) held an exhibition of Akira's work, which has appeared on the catwalks of Paris and is stocked in top boutiques in 12 countries.

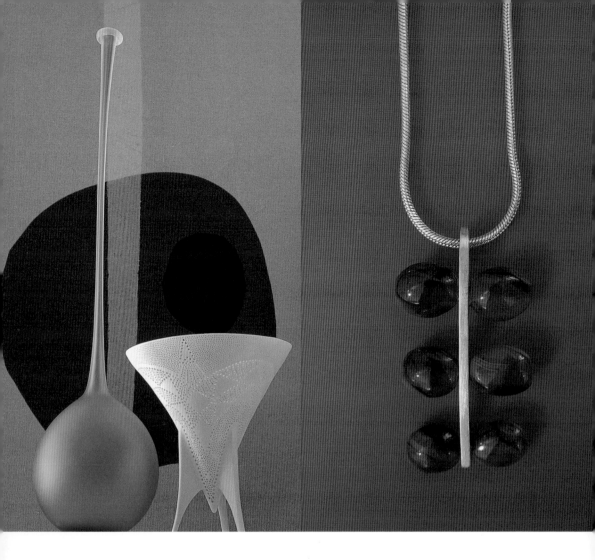

14 **Object Store**

13 88 George Street

For 40 years the Object organization's mission has been to increase the visibility and viability of contemporary craft and design in Australia. Their annual shows and exhibitions, which have featured the likes of Dinosaur Designs and Akira Isogawa, serve to support new and emerging talent. Recent designers who promise big things include Edward Wong, whose wares were showcased at the Milan Furniture Fair in 2001 and 2002. The Object Store in the Rocks is their shop selling the best in Australian design,

where you can find beautiful, strikingly original ceramics, glassware, fabrics and jewelry. Their gallery, which used to be in Customs House at Circular Quay, is reopening in 2004 in the former chapel of St Margaret's Hospital, Surry Hills. The chapel, designed by eminent Australian architect Ken Woolley in 1958 is being given a makeover by award-winning Sam Marshall and promises to be one of the best exhibition spaces in Sydney.

54 **Customweave Carpets & Rugs**

13 499 Crown Street

Two butterflies – one pine the other jarrah wood – flap their wings across a chocolate alpaca wool carpet studded with slender leather tassles. A Japanese–style floral design by eminent Australian printed wallpaper designer Florence Broadhurst (1899–1977) rendered in wool, silk, leather and lurex. The custom-made carpets and rugs of Customweave are so beautiful and unusual that you'll be more likely to hang them on the wall than spread them on the floor. They are all locally made using Australian wool and can be ordered in a full spectrum of natural dyes. The company has sole rights to use Broadhurst's classic portfolio of floral and geometric print designs on carpets and rugs but, while the visual appearance of the carpet is important to the Melbourne-based company, it is the quality and feel of the texture that is paramount.

64 **Hogarth Galleries**

4 7 Walker Lane

Both ancient and modern, Aboriginal art is one of the most distinctive creative forms to have come out of Australia in the past 30 years. Visual imagery is a fundamental part of Australian indigenous life, dating back 30,000 years, but it wasn't until the early 1970s that a wider national and international audience began to take note. At the forefront of bringing the cream of indigenous art to world attention has been Paddington's Hogarth Galleries. The spacious gallery, which hosts regularly changing exhibitions, works with communities across Australia to support emerging artists and promote successful ones. Their diverse stock includes paintings on bark, canvas and wood, baskets woven from vegetable-dyed pandanus fibre, traditional conical mats from central Arnhem Land and artifacts such as ceremonial shields and spear throwers. The gallery also has shops on George Street in the Rocks, opposite the Museum of Contemporary Art, and next to the stage door of the Sydney Opera House.

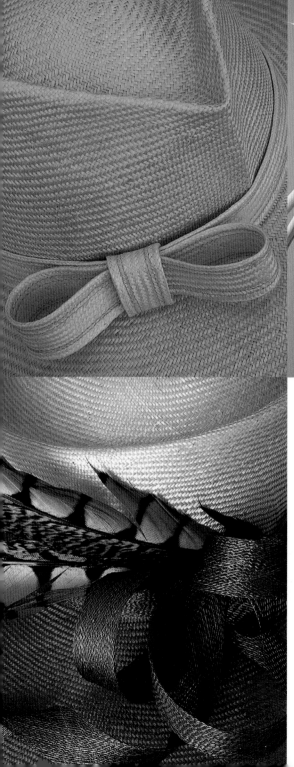

Nerida Winter

21 10/20 Bay Street

When Gai Waterhouse, the horse-trainer queen of the Australian race track, wants a new hat she goes to Nerida Winter, the Double Bay emporium of the Sydney-born milliner, Nerida, who trained in Sydney and worked in the US during the early 1990s. She began to gain a reputation while working with designer Isabella Klompé at the same shop, and took over the business in 2003, which now offers eye-catching designs in the brightest, most fashion-conscious palette of colours. What really sets her raw fibre hats apart, though, is the attention to detail – hand-curled feathers, painted quills or beaded spines of feathers – and her love of putting a modern twist on classic pieces, such as her favourite 1980s–style cocktail pillbox with antique netting. Brilliant headpieces of feathers or flowers floating on combs also feature in her collection.

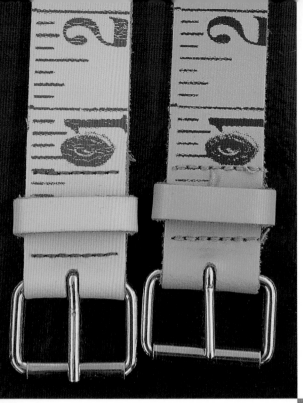

Australia's quintessential gemstone is the opal. More than 95 per cent of the world's opals are mined here and every one of the brilliantly coloured clusters of hydrated silica are unique, making them as interesting as diamonds, emeralds and rubies. Shops selling cut and polished opals, both as individual stones or in jewelry settings, abound in Sydney, and many are clustered in the Rocks. Opal Fields is the best if you're looking for unique and contemporary jewelry designs to complement these stones that reflect all the colours of the spectrum. Beautiful pieces by award-winning designers such as Diane Appleby and Taka Morino incorporate black, milky white and rare Queensland boulder opals into distinctive gold and silver settings.

ONE STOP STYLE

`54` **Orson & Blake**

`14` 483 Riley Street

Orson & Blake, brainchild of mother and son Mandy and David Heimann, began life in 1992 as a small store in Woollahra selling well-designed but affordable homewares and women's clothes, inspired by Terence Conran's shops in London. Their vision caught on and today, as well as bigger premises in Woollahra, they have this major showroom in Surry Hills. Combining furniture from leading Australian designers and manufacturers, a basement of cutting-edge fashion, gallery space, a bookshop and a very decent café, you could easily spend a couple of hours exploring and indulging in their brand of eclecticism. Organic-shaped ceramics by Elliot Go Lightly and David Edmunds, Senufu African stools, bone-inlaid tables from Morocco, cowhide rugs and luxurious leather ottomans are all fit for a style magazine shoot. Head to the basement to find hip T-shirts by Flux, Shakuhachi and Saviour, artfully distressed jeans by tsubi and cute Lucky Beggar coffee-cup shaped purses from New York.

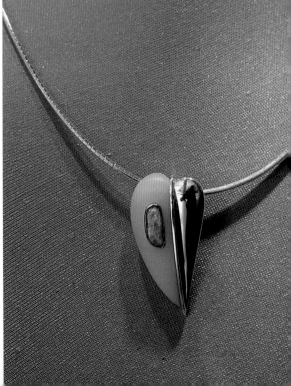

FUNKY CHUNKY
28 Dinosaur Designs
9 Strand Arcade, 412–14 George Street, shop 77

Formed in 1985 by Sydney art-school friends Louise Olsen, Stephen Ormandy and Liane Rossler, Dinosaur Designs, like many other Sydney retailing successes, got their break at Paddington Market (p. 69). Now their main retail store is in the CBD's Strand Arcade and the other is a distinctive, multicoloured presence on Oxford Street's golden mile of shops. The team's moulded resin desirable homewares, jewelry and decorative objects are applauded by design afficionados worldwide for their bold use of colours – everything from snowy white and clear to swirly celadon and tortoiseshell – and chunky, organic forms. They also have a distinctly Australian character, with many of their colours and forms evoking the country's vibrant natural landscape. Inspiration comes from a wide range of sources: their early jewelry designs featured retro spaceships and robots and prehistoric creatures, and their salad bowl and servers are Australian design icons. More abstract designs have been inspired by artists Henry Moore, Jackson Pollock and Mark Rothko, not to mention the Flintstones.

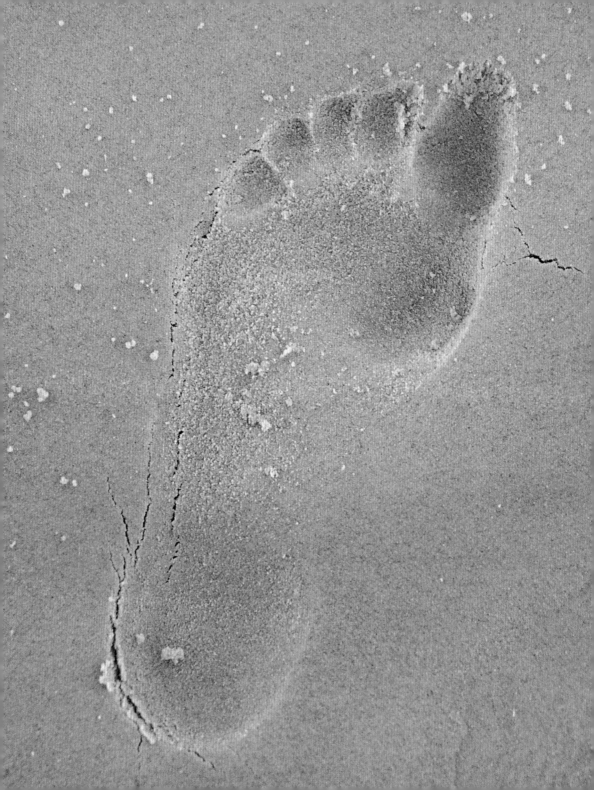

retreat

It's hard to imagine wanting to escape somewhere as appealing and laid-back as Sydney — until you discover the amazing retreats practically on the doorstep. These four destinations each capture a different aspect of the Australian experience: climb aboard a seaplane at Rose Bay for a scenic flight to the sandy pleasures of Palm Beach and Pittwater, or the river paradise of Hawkesbury River. Hunter Valley, Australia's oldest wine-growing region, is the place to sample some very fine vintages in verdant countryside. Or head to the Blue Mountains where the eucalyptus-scented air will spark your appetite for outdoor adventure and the inventive cuisine of the area.

The Hawkesbury River: Unwinding in the Bush

- Oxley Boatshed
- Riverside Brooklyn Restaurant
- Peats Bite

Even on a rainy day the Hawkesbury River is magnificent. Weathered sandstone cliffs and rocks with the appearance of melted wax, clad with eucalyptus and grassy mop-headed xanthria, border a twisting river flowing out to Barrenjoey Heads and the Pacific Ocean. One can imagine this is how Sydney looked before the European settlers arrived and when the land was occupied by the Ku-ring-gai people whose carvings are found in 2000 known sites along the river. Most incredibly it's less than an hour's drive or train ride north of the city to the river's main settlement of Brooklyn, a community of 750 people living in serene proximity to seven national parks and three nature reserves.

This abundance of protected bush, and the fact that to get practically anywhere near the river you need a boat, has kept development to the absolute minimum. There are no hotels, just calmly floating houseboats and holiday cottages for let, all with waterviews and immediate river access from private jetties. Unassuming from the outside, Oxley's Boatshed, a weatherboard and timber converted boatshed dating from 1924, is a revelation. The artfully renovated space reflects owner Rosyln Oxley's philosophy of 'less design, more character'. The rough hewn central fireplace contrasts with beaten antique leather club chairs, Art-Déco lamps, stained-glass windows and a collection of striking Aboriginal art. Guests at this ultimate chill-out zone will immediately feel relaxed and will not want to leave – ever.

Visitors can hire a 'tinnie' (tin boat) and putter upriver to Marramarra creek where contorted mangroves rise up from the emerald-tinted water. Sydney rock oysters from the river figure on the menus of local restaurants, including the Riverside Brooklyn Restaurant – try them as creamy as nature intended or with wasabi vinagrette, pickled ginger and flying fish roe. Another great place to lose an afternoon over fine food and wine is the water-access only Peats Bite, where you may need to dodge the swallows swooping into their nest in the bar.

The Hunter Valley: Evolution of the Vineyards

- Tower Lodge
- Tempus Two
- Roberts at Pepper Tree
- Tower Estate

The Hunter Valley, two-and-a-half hours drive north of Sydney, is Australia's oldest wine growing region, home to 50 wineries. Beautiful rolling pastures have been grooved with vines since 1824, its western flank rising up in the eucalyptus clad slopes of the Great Dividing Range. Millions of dollars have recently been ploughed into striking developments such as the luxurious boutique hotel Tower Lodge and the hyper-modern winery and Japanese–Thai restaurant Tempus Two, which pushes the Hunter Valley's evolution to a contemporary design-focused level.

It's easy to see why Robert's at Pepper Tree in Pokolbin, run by the genial Algerian-born chef Robert Molines and his engaging Australian wife Sally, is considered a benchmark for cuisine and hospitality in the region. The restaurant, nestling behind an ironbark cottage dating from 1876, is decorated with battered leather chairs, lavish sprays of flowers and an Afro–Amish quilt. Molines specializes in what he calls 'cuisine de terroir', food that utilizes the best of the region's produce, including fresh seafood from nearby Port Stephens, best partnered with a semillion wine for which the Hunter is renown.

Robert's is now part of Tower Estate, which includes a boutique winery known for individual wines made from the best grapes from across Australia. Its architectural style – Mediterranean with Australian twists – is echoed up the road at Tower Lodge, where a pair of monumental French coach house doors lead the way into the Hunter's most eccentrically designed accommodation. Each of the 12 airy guestrooms has its own décor, prompting lively conversation over the hearty breakfast served around the communal table in the grand baronial dining room. Did you sleep in the 300-year-old hand-carved Rajasthani bed in the Chairman's suite or share a bubble bath in the plunge pool in the oriental room? It makes a change from swapping wine notes, the usual Hunter Valley small talk.

Katoomba, Leura & Blackheath: Food with Altitude
- Silk's
- Echoes Boutique Hotel & Restaurant
- Vulcans

Mother nature's grand design is writ large across the Blue Mountains, two hours west of Sydney by road or rail. Rising to 1300 metres at its highest point, the park's 85-kilometre-wide sandstone plateau has been etched and eroded over the millennia to create gaping valleys, sheer cliffs and deep, mysterious ravines. It is an Australian symphony of plunging canyons blanketed with the eucaplytus trees whose oil, floating as a fine mist in the air, conjures the distinctive blue haze that gives the area its name. Epic vistas and unique vegetation make the mountains a mecca for outdoor adventurers, whether hiking and exploring the canyons, or absailing and rock climbing the lichen-splattered sandstone cliffs. All that activity is guaranteed to sharpen the appetite, so it's just as well the Blue Mountains have several award-winning restaurants, convivial cafés and cosy lodgings with a welcome as warm as their obligatory log fires.

In stylish, old-money Leura, Silk's Brasserie eschews the Mountains' reputation for ruffles and chintz in favour of contemporary design in both décor and cuisine. Combine the succulent sautéed duck liver, black pudding and handmade gnocchi, or the heavenly light curd cheesecake made with milk from the local Jannei creamery, with wine from its top-class list.

In Katoomba, Echoes, an intimate 12-room boutique hotel and restaurant close to the iconic rock known as the Three Sisters, also ditches the area's twee style in favour of something more of the moment. The monochrome décor and contemporary take on Federation-era architecture play second fiddle, though, to its finest feature: sweeping views of the Jamison Valley.

Just when you think the vistas couldn't get any better, head a few kilometres further west to Blackheath, the village closest to Govetts Leap and the breathtaking panorama across the Grosse Valley. Equally memorable is a meal at Vulcans; the utilitarian décor of this former bakery give little hint of the legendary culinary creations of chef Philip Searle.

Pittwater, Avalon, Newport, Palm Beach: Style by the Sea

- Swell
- Rockridge
- Jonah's
- Dish

The recipe for the perfect Sydney beach trip: grab your sun glasses, swimming costume and sun screen and head a mere 40 kilometres north of the city centre where the surf's a ripper, so if you have a board you might want to bring that too. There's no need to worry about a packed lunch; there are plenty of great dining options, kicking off with Swell. This simple box-like space on Old Barrenjoey Road, near Avalon's rusty red beach, is the place to go for breakfast or lunch. Try avocado and leafy coriander on toast or a scrumptious plate of Belgium waffles with orange ricotta and maple syrup.

Avalon and its neighbouring northern beachside suburbs of Newport and Palm Beach are known locally as the insular peninsula. Some of Sydney's most desirable real estate is ranged across a rocky strip of land separating the mighty Pacific and its pounding surf from placid Pittwater and the sandstone outcrops, inlets and coves of Ku-ring-gai Chase National Park. A ferry from Palm Beach's pretty-as-a-picture wharf takes you to secluded beaches and bush trails in the park, or you could hire boats or kayaks to sail and paddle around Pittwater itself. Several weekender cottages in the area are available to rent, including Rockridge with a commanding position overlooking Palm Beach. This weatherbeaten timber-and-stone house has a shabby-chic interior that encapsulates the Pittwater aesthetic – a look you can recreate from the boutiques along Barrenjoey Road.

Another place to stay is 65 Bynya Road, the B&B adjoining historic Jonah's, a restaurant that has had the best views of Whale Beach (and the passing pods of whales) since 1928. The menu is old-school Palm Beach – classic fish dishes and comforting desserts. More contemporary is Dish in Newport where San Franciscan chef George Francisco's fabulous seafood dishes have created waves. His desserts are pretty good too – the blood-orange parfait is reminiscent of the juiciest iced lolly on the beach.

contact

All telephone numbers are given for dialling locally: the country code for Australia is +61; the code for New South Wales is 02. Therefore, when dialling from abroad, dial +612 followed by the eight digit number. The number in brackets by the name is the page number on which the entry appears.

The ABC Shop [33]
Shop 48, QVB, 555 George Street
CBD, Sydney 2000
T 9286 3726

Akira [169]
12a Queen Street
Woollahra, Sydney 2025
T 9361 5221
E akirashop@thedoor.com.au
W www.akira.au.com

Alannah Hill [33/66]
Shop 50, Strand Arcade
412–14 George Street
CBD, Sydney 2000
T 9221 1251
118–120 Oxford Street
Paddington, Sydney 2021
T 9380 9147

Alfies [78]
85 Gould Street
Bondi, Sydney 2026
T 9300 6466

Alistair Trung [19]
Level 1, Argyle Stores
18–24 Argyle Street
The Rocks, Sydney 2000
T/F 9252 8828
W www.alistairtrung.com

Andrew (Boy) Charlton Pool [44]
1c Mrs Macquaries Road
Woolloomooloo, Sydney 2000
T 9358 6686
F 9358 6540
W www.abcpool.org

Andrew McDonald [163]
58 William Street
Paddington, Sydney 2021
T 9358 6793

E amcshoe@yahoo.com
W www.andrewmcdonald.com.au

Aqua Dining [98]
Corner Paul & Northcliff Streets
Milsons Point, Sydney 2061
T 9964 9998
E reservations@aquadining.com.au
W www.aquadining.com.au

Aqua Luna [22]
5–7 Macquarie Street
Circular Quay, Sydney 2000
T 9251 0311
F 9251 0322
W www.aqualuna.com.au

Architext [47]
3 Manning Street
Potts Point, Sydney 2011
T 9356 2022
F 9368 1570
E sydney@architext.com.au
W www.architext.com.au

Aria [22]
1 Macquarie Street
Circular Quay, Sydney 2000
T 9252 2555
F 9252 2666
E mail@ariarestaurant.com
W www.ariarestaurant.com

Arida [48]
61 Macleay Street
Potts Point, Sydney 2011
T 9357 4788

Art Gallery of New South Wales [45]
Art Gallery Road
Woolloomooloo, Sydney 2000
T 9225 1740
   restaurant: 9225 1819

E artmail@ag.nsw.gov.au
W www.artgallery.nsw.gov.au

Arte Flowers [70]
112 Queen Street
Woollahra, Sydney 2025
T 9328 0402
W www.arteflowers.com

Athol Hall [102]
Ashton Park, Bradleys Head Road
Mosman, Sydney 2088
T 9968 4441

Australian Centre for Photography [66]
257 Oxford Street
Paddington, Sydney 2021
T 9332 1455
F 9331 6887
W www.acp.au.com

Australian Image Craft & Telopea Gallery Craft [21]
Shop 2, Metcalf Arcade
80–88 George Street
The Rocks, Sydney 2000
T 9241 5825 / 9241 1673
E gallery@artsandcraftsnsw.com.au
W www.artsandcraftsnsw.com.au

Australian National Maritime Museum [34]
2 Murray Street
Darling Harbour, Sydney 2009
T 9298 3777
F 9298 3655
W www.anmm.gov.au

Awaba [102]
67 The Esplanade
Balmoral, Sydney 2088
T 9969 2104
W www.awabacafe.com.au

Badde Manors [88]
37 Glebe Point Road
Glebe, Sydney 2037
T 9660 3797

Balmain Markets [93]
St Andrew's Congregational Church,
Corner Darling Street & Curtis Road
Balmain, Sydney 2041

Bambini Trust Cafe [38]
185 Elizabeth Street
CBD, Sydney 2000
T 9283 7098

Bank Hotel [88]
324 King Street
Newtown, Sydney 2042
T 9557 1692

Bar Coluzzi [51]
322 Victoria Street
Darlinghurst, Sydney 2010
T 9380 5420

Bar Italia [91]
169–71 Norton Street
Leichhardt, Sydney 2040
T 9560 9981

Baron's [48]
5 Rosyln Street
King's Cross, Sydney 2011
T 9358 6131

Bathers' Pavilion Restaurant & Cafe [143]
4 The Esplanade
Balmoral, Sydney 2088
T 9969 5050
F 9969 4626
E eat@batherspavilion.com.au
W www.batherspavilion.com.au

 186 contact

Bayswater Brasserie [48]
32 Bayswater Road
King's Cross, Sydney 2011
T   9357 2177
F   9358 1213
E   brasserie@ozemail.com.au
W   www.bayswaterbrasserie.com.au

BBQ King [37]
18–20 Goulburn Street
Haymarket, Sydney 2000
T   9267 2586

Bécasse [61]
48 Albion Street
Surry Hills, Sydney 2010
T   9280 3202
W   www.becasse.com.au

bel mondo [19]
Level 3, Argyle Stores
18–24 Argyle Street
The Rocks, Sydney 2000
T   9241 3700
F   9241 3744
E   reservations@belmondo.com.au
W   www.belmondo.com.au

Belinda [68/70]
39 William Street
Paddington, Sydney 2021
T   9380 8728
8 Transvaal Avenue
Double Bay, Sydney 2028
T   9328 6288
W   www.belinda.com.au

Belle Fleur [93]
658 Darling Street
Rozelle, Sydney 2039
T   9810 2690
E   info@bellefleur.com.au
W   www.bellefleur.com.au

Belvoir Street Theatre [61]
25 Belvoir Street
Surry Hills, Sydney 2010
T   9699 3444
E   mail@belvoir.com.au
W   www.belvoir.com.au

Beowulf Galleries [70]
23 Queen Street
Woollahra, Sydney 2025
T   9362 5583
F   9362 5586
E   beowulfgalleries@
    ozemail.com.au
W   www.beowulfgalleries.com.au

Berkelouw's Books [91]
70 Norton Street
Leichhardt, Sydney 2040
T   9560 3200
F   9564 8511
E   books@berkelouw.com.au
W   www.berkelouw.com.au

Bettina Liano [33]
Shops 74–78, Strand Arcade
412–14 George Street
CBD, Sydney 2000
T   9223 3511
W   www.bettinaliano.com.au

Big Boys Giftshop & Cafe [90]
106 Erskineville Road
Erskineville, Sydney 2043
T   9557 9448

bills [146]
433 Liverpool Street
Darlinghurst, Sydney 2010
T   9360 9631
bills 2
359 Crown Sreet
Surry Hills, Sydney 2010
T   9360 4762

Billy Kwong [58]
355 Crown Street, shop 3
Surry Hills, Sydney 2010
T   9332 3300

Bistro Lulu [66]
257 Oxford Street
Paddington, Sydney 2021
T   9380 6888
E   info@bistrolulu.com.au
W   www.bistrolulu.com.au

Bistro Moncur [138]
The Woollahra Hotel
116 Queen Street
Woollahra, Sydney 2025
T   9363 2519
W   www.woollahrahotel.com.au

Blue Ginger [93]
241 Darling Street
Balmain, Sydney 2041
T   9818 4662
W   www.blueginger.com.au

**The Boathouse Blackwattle
Bay** [142]
End of Ferry Road
Glebe, Sydney 2037
T   9518 9011
F   9518 9098
E   boathouse@ozemail.com.au
W   www.bluewaterboathouse.com.au

Booker's [66]
209–11 Glenmore Road
Paddington, Sydney 2021
T   9332 3328

The Bookshop Darlinghurst [57]
207 Oxford Street
Darlinghurst, Sydney 2010
T   9331 1103
E   info@thebookshop.com.au
W   www.thebookshop.com.au

**Bottom of the Harbour
Antiques** [20]
104 George Street
The Rocks, Sydney 2000
T   9247 8107

Bracewell [66]
274 Oxford Street
Paddington, Sydney 2021
T   9331 5844
W   www.bracewell.com.au

Brett Whiteley Studio [61]
2 Raper Street
Surry Hills, Sydney 2010
T   9225 1740
F   9221 5129
E   brettwhiteleystudio@
    ag.nsw.gov.au
W   www.brettwhiteley.org

Bridge Bar [22]
Level 10, 3 Macquarie Street
Circular Quay, Sydney 2000
T   9252 6800
F   9252 9600
E   info@bridgebar.com.au
W   www.bridgebar.com.au

BridgeClimb [16]
5 Cumberland Street
The Rocks, Sydney 2000
T   8274 7777
W   www.bridgeclimb.com

Bronte House [82]
470 Bronte Road
Bronte, Sydney 2024
W   www.brontehouse.com.au

Brown Sugar [147]
100 Brighton Boulevard
Bondi, Sydney 2026
T   9365 6262

Bruno Dutot [51]
120A Darlinghurst Road
Darlinghurst, Sydney 2010
T   0425 305 570

Cadman's Cottage [25]
Sydney Harbour National Park
Information Centre
110 George Street
The Rocks, Sydney 2000
T   9247 5033
W   www.nationalparks.nsw.gov.au

Café Mint [58]
579 Crown Street
Surry Hills, Sydney 2010
T   9319 0848
W   www.cafemint.com.au

Café Sydney [17]
Level 5, Customs House
31 Alfred Street
Circular Quay, Sydney 2000
T   9251 8683
F   9251 8363
W   www.cafesydney.com

Café Zoe [61]
688 Bourke Street
Redfern, Sydney 2016
T   8399 0940

Calibre [38]
139 Elizabeth Street
CBD, Sydney 2000
T   9267 9321
E   info@calibreclothing.com.au
W   www.calibreclothing.com.au

Campos [88]
193 Missenden Road
Newtown, Sydney 2042
T   9516 3361

Canteen [93]
332 Darling Street
Balmain, Sydney 2041
T   9818 1521

Cargo Bar [34]
52–60 The Promenade
Kings Street Wharf
Darling Harbour, Sydney 2000
T   9262 1777
F   9262 1733
W   www.cargobar.com.au

Catalina Rose Bay [139]
1 Sunderland Avenue
Rose Bay, Sydney 2029
T   9371 0555
F   9371 0559
E   reservations@
    catalinarosebay.com.au
W   www.catalinarosebay.com.au

Centennial Park [69]
Paddington, Sydney 2021
T   9339 6699
E   info@cp.nsw.gov.au
W   www.cp.nsw.gov.au

Chaos Cafe [99]
194 Military Road
Neutral Bay, Sydney 2089
T   9953 8625

Chee Soon & Fitzgerald [58]
387 Crown Street
Surry Hills, Sydney 2010
T   9360 1031
W   www.cheesoonfitzgerald.com

The Chelsea [120]
49 Womerah Avenue
Darlinghurst, Sydney 2010
T   9380 5994
F   9332 2491
E   xchelsea@ozemail.com.au
W   www.chelsea.citysearch.com.au

**Chetcuti Boutique – Coco
Monkey Interiors** [58]
340 Crown Street
Surry Hills, Sydney 2010
T   9358 1966

Chicane [156]
1A Burton Street
Darlinghurst, Sydney 2010
T   9380 2121
F   9380 9766
E   dining@chicane.com.au
W   www.chicane.com.au

Chinese Noodle Restaurant [37]
8 Quay Street
Haymarket, Sydney 2000
T   9281 9051

Chinta Ria...Temple of Love [34]
The Roof Terrace, Cockle Bay Wharf
201 Sussex Street
Darling Harbour, Sydney 2000
T   9264 3211

Christensen Copenhagen [73]
2 Guilfoyle Avenue
Double Bay, Sydney 2028
T   9328 9755
F   9362 9165
E   mail@christensen
    copenhagen.com.au
W   www.christensen
    copenhagen.com.au

Civic [151]
388 Pitt Street
CBD, Sydney 2000
T   8080 7000
F   8080 7001
W   www.civichotel.com.au

Claude's [138]
10 Oxford Street
Woollahra, Sydney 2025
T   9331 2325
E   bookings@claudes.org
W   www.claudes.org

Clifford Gordon [66]
466 Oxford Street
Paddington, Sydney 2021
T   9360 3477

Clock Hotel [58]
470 Crown Street
Surry Hills, Sydney 2010
T   9331 5333
F   9380 7966
E   enquiries@clockhotel.com.au
W   www.greenwoodhotel.com.au/
    clock

Cloth [166]
207 Clovelly Road
Clovelly, Sydney 2031
T   9664 5570
E   cloth@clothfabric.com
W   www.clothfabric.com

Coast [34]
The Roof Terrace, Cockle Bay Wharf
201 Sussex Street
Darling Harbour, Sydney 2000
T   9267 6700
W   www.coastrestaurant.com.au

Coco Nobué [33]
Shop 20, Strand Arcade
412–14 George Street
CBD, Sydney 2000
T   9233 1233

Collette Dinnigan [160]
33 William Street
Paddington, Sydney 2021
T   9360 6691
F   9361 6215

E cdsydney@
collettedinnigan.com.au
W www.collettedinnigan.com.au

The Columbian [57]
117–23 Oxford Street
Surry Hills, Sydney 2010
T 9360 2151

Country Road [99]
742 Military Road
Mosman, Sydney 2088
T 9960 4633
W www.countryroad.com.au

Cruise [22]
Level 1, Overseas
Passenger Terminal
Circular Quay, Sydney 2000
T 9251 1188
W www.cruisebar.tv

Crumpler [66]
30 Oxford Street
Paddington, Sydney 2021
T 9331 4660
E enquiries@crumpler.com.au
W www.crumpler.com.au

**Customweave Carpets
& Rugs** [171]
499 Crown Street
Surry Hills, Sydney 2010
T 9699 2499
E sydney@customweave.com.au
W www.customweave.com.au

Danks Street Depot [146]
2 Danks Street
Waterloo, Sydney 2017
T 9698 2201

Darlo Bar [51]
Royal Sovereign Hotel
Corner Darlinghurst Road &
Liverpool Street
Darlinghurst, Sydney 2010
T 9331 3672
W www.darlobar.com

David Jones [161]
86–108 Castlereagh Street
CBD, Sydney 2000
T 9266 5544
F 9267 7326
W www.davidjones.com.au

de Cjuba [51]
314–18 Victoria Street
Darlinghurst, Sydney 2010
T 9380 4056

Déclic [66]
450 Oxford Street
Paddington, Sydney 2021
T 9361 6662
W www.declic.com.au

The Dendy [22]
Shop 9, 2 East Circular Quay
Circular Quay, Sydney 2000
T 9247 3800
E opera@dendy.com.au
W www.dendy.com.au

Dinosaur Designs [175]
Shop 77, Strand Arcade
412–14 George Street
CBD, Sydney 2000
T 9223 2953
339 Oxford Street
Paddington, Sydney 2021
T 9361 3776
E dinosaur@
dinosaurdesigns.com.au
W www.dinosaurdesigns.com.au

Don Adán Coffee House [150]
5 Spit Road, shop 2

Mosman, Sydney 2088
T 9968 2828

Doyles [22/78]
Doyles at the Quay
Level 1, Overseas Passenger
Terminal
Circular Quay, Sydney 2000
T 9252 3400
Doyles Palace Hotel
1 Military Road
Watsons Bay, Sydney 2030
T 9337 5444
Doyles on the Beach
11 Marine Parde
Watsons Bay, Sydney 2030
T 9337 2007
W www.doyles.com.au

Dragstar [81]
96 Glenayr Avenue, shop 2
Bondi, Sydney 2026
T 9365 2244
W www.dragstar.com.au

East Ocean [37]
421–29 Sussex Street
Haymarket, Sydney 2000
T 9212 4198

East Sydney Hotel [47]
Cornor Crown & Cathedral Streets
Woolloomooloo, Sydney 2010
T 9358 1975

Ecabar [51]
128 Darlinghurst Road
Darlinghurst, Sydney 2010
T 9332 1433

ECQ [22]
Grand Quay Hotel
63 Macquarie Street
Circular Quay, Sydney 2000
T 9256 4000

Edna's Table [133]
204 Clarence Street
CBD, Sydney 2000
T 9267 3933
F 9264 9002
E ednas@acay.com.au
W www.ednastable.com

Electric Monkeys [78]
78 Gould Street
Bondi, Sydney 2026
T 9365 6955
W www.electricmonkeys.com

Elio [91]
159 Norton Street
Leichhardt, Sydney 2040
T 9560 9129
F 9568 1348
W www.elio.com.au

Elizabeth Bay House [48]
7 Onslow Avenue
Elizabeth Bay, Sydney 2011
T 9356 3022
F 9357 7176
E info@hht.net.au
W www.hht.nsw.gov.au

Emma's on Liberty [90]
59 Liberty Street
Enmore, Sydney 2042
T/F 9550 3458
W www.emmasonliberty.com.au

Empire [72]
2 Guilfoyle Avenue, shop 2
Double Bay, Sydney 2028
T 9328 7556

Enmore Theatre [90]
130 Enmore Road
Enmore, Sydney 2042

T 9550 3666
F 9550 2990
E admin@enmoretheatre.com.au
W www.enmoretheatre.com.au

The Essential Ingredient [93]
4 Australia Street
Camperdown, Sydney 2050
T 9550 5477

Est. [131]
Establishment Hotel
252 George Street
CBD, Sydney 2000
T 9240 3010
E info@establishmenthotel.com
W www.establishmenthotel.com

Establishment [112]
5 Bridge Lane
CBD, Sydney 2000
T 9240 3100
F 9240 3101
E info@establishmenthotel.com
W www.establishmenthotel.com

Faster Pussycat [88]
431A King Street
Newtown, Sydney 2042
T/F 9519 1744
W www.fasterpussycatonline.com

Fishface [51]
132 Darlinghurst Road
Darlinghurst, Sydney 2010
T 9332 4803
E info@fishface.com.au
W www.fishface.com.au

Five Ways Cellars [66]
4 Heeley Street
Paddington, Sydney 2021
T 9360 4242

Forty One [31]
Chifley Tower, 2 Chifley Square
CBD, Sydney 2000
T 9221 2500
E reservations@forty-one.com.au
W www.forty-one.com.au

Fratelli Paradiso [48]
12-16 Challis Avenue
Potts Point, Sydney 2011
T 9357 1744

Fresh Ketch [102]
77a Parriwi Road
Mosman, Sydney 2088
T 9969 5665
F 9960 4836
E bookings@freshketch.com.au
W www.freshketch.com.au

...from St Xavier [78]
75a Gould Street
Bondi, Sydney 2026
T 9365 4644
F 9365 4512
E crew@fromstxavier.com
W www.fromstxavier.com

Funkis [81]
23c Curlewis Street
Bondi, Sydney 2026
T 9130 6445
E bondi@funkis.com
Strand Arcade
412–14 George Street
CBD, Sydney 2000
T 9221 9370
E strand@funkis.com
W www.funkis.com

**G&L Handmade Shoe
Designers** [68]
3 William Street
Paddington, Sydney 2021

T 8354 1005
W www.glbros.com

Gallery 4A [37]
181–87 Hay Street
Haymarket, Sydney 2000
T 9212 0380
F 9281 0873
E info@4a.com.au
W www.4a.com.au

Gallery Onefivesix [58]
156 Commonwealth Street
Surry Hills, Sydney 2010
T 9280 4156
F 9280 4050
W www.onefivesix.net

Gallery Serpentine [90]
123 Enmore Road
Enmore, Sydney 2042
T 9557 5821
W www.galleryserpentine.com.au

Garfish [98]
21 Broughton Street, shop 2
Kirribilli, Sydney 2061
T 9922 4322
F 9922 4189
E info@garfish.com.au
W www.garfish.com.au

Gavala Aboriginal Art [34]
Harbourside Shopping Centre
Darling Harbour, Sydney 2009
T 9212 7232
E info@gavala.com.au
W www.gavala.com.au

Gertrude & Alice [81]
40 Hall Street
Bondi, Sydney 2026
T 9130 5155

Glamourpuss [169]
58 Darley Road
Manly, Sydney 2095
T 9977 5826
F 9977 5865
W www.glamourpuss.com.au

Glebe Market [88]
Glebe Public School
Glebe Point Road
Glebe, Sydney 2037
T 4237 7499

Gleebooks [88]
49 Glebe Point Road
Glebe, Sydney 2037
T 9660 2333
F 960 3597
W www.gleebooks.com.au

Gosh [93]
297 Darling Street
Balmain, Sydney 2041
T 9555 8400

Gould's Book Arcade [88]
32–38 King Street
Newtown, Sydney 2042
T 9519 8947

Gowings [165]
45 Market Street
CBD, Sydney 2000
T 9287 6394
W www.gowings.com.au

Grain Interior [99]
527 Military Road
Mosman, Sydney 2088
T 9969 9282
E sales@graininterior.com.au
W www.graininterior.com.au

Green's Café [81]
140 Glenayr Avenue
Bondi, Sydney 2026
T   9130 6181

Ground Zero [105]
Shop 2, 18 Sydney Road
Manly, Sydney 2095
T   9977 6996

Guillaume at Bennelong [152]
Sydney Opera House
Bennelong Point
Circular Quay, Sydney 2000
T   9241 1999
F   9241 3795
E   enquiries@
    guillaumeatbennelong.com.au
W   www.guillaumeat
    bennelong.com.au

Gusto [66]
Corner Broughton & Heeley Streets
Paddington, Sydney 2021
T   9361 5640

Hanksta [58]
346 Crown Street
Surry Hills, Sydney 2010
T   9360 7253
E   loveis@hanksta.com
W   www.hanksta.com

harbourkitchen&bar [22]
Park Hyatt Hotel, 7 Hickson Road
The Rocks, Sydney 2000
T   9256 1661
F   9256 1445
W   www.harbourkitchen.com.au

Harry's Café de Wheels [44]
Cowper Wharf Road
Woolloomooloo, Sydney 2011
T   9357 3074
W   www.harryscafedewheels.com.au

The Hayden Orpheum Picture Palace [99]
380 Military Road
Cremorne, Sydney 2090
T   9908 4344
W   www.orpheum.com.au

Helen Kaminski [19]
Argyle Stores, 18–24 Argyle Street
The Rocks, Sydney 2000
T   9251 9850
W   www.helenkaminski.com

Hemmesphere [152]
Level 4, Establishment
252 George Street
CBD, Sydney 2000
T   9240 3040
F   9240 3002
E   info@establishmenthotel.com
W   www.establishmenthotel.com

Herringbone [33]
Shop 25, QVB, 455 George Street
CBD, Sydney 2000
T   9266 0500
W   www.herringbone.com.au

Hogarth Galleries [172]
7 Walker Lane
Paddington, Sydney 2021
T   9360 6839
F   9360 7069
E   hogarthgal@bigpond.com
W   www.aboriginalartcentres.com

Höglund Art Glass Gallery [70]
92 Queen Street
Woollahra, Sydney 2025
T   9326 1556
E   sydney-gallery@hoglund.com.au
W   www.sydney.hoglund.com.au

The House of Green [47]
84–85 Nicholson Street
Woolloomooloo, Sydney 2011
T   9360 7444

House of Shanghai [51]
171 Palmer Street
Darlinghurst, Sydney 2010
T   9357 4092

The Hughenden [70]
14 Queen Street
Woollahra, Sydney 2025
T   9363 4863
E   admin@hughendenhotel.com.au
W   www.hughendenhotel.com.au

Hugo's [82]
70 Campbell Parade
Bondi, Sydney 2026
T   9300 0900
W   www.hugos.com.au

Hugo's Lounge [48]
Level 1, 33 Bayswater Road
Kings Cross, Sydney 2011
T   9357 4411
W   www.hugos.com.au

Icebergs Dining Room & Bar [140]
1 Notts Avenue
Bondi, Sydney 2026
T   9365 9000
F   9365 9099
E   idrb@idrb.com
W   www.idrb.com

Ichi-Ban Boshi [33]
Shop 129, Strand Arcade
412–14 George Street
CBD, Sydney 2000
T   9221 6838

Imperial Hotel [90]
35 Erskinville Road
Erskinville, Sydney 2043
T   9519 9899

Infinity Sourdough Bakery [51]
225 Victoria Street
Darlinghurst, Sydney 2010
T   9380 4320

Jeremy Store [66]
26 Oxford Street
Paddington, Sydney 2021
T   9332 1526
E   info@jeremyville.com
W   www.jeremyville.com

jimmy liks [156]
186–88 Victoria Street
Potts Point, Sydney 2011
T   8354 1400

Johnston & Bell [93]
364 Darling Street
Balmain, Sydney 2041
T   9555 1031

jones the grocer [70]
68 Moncur Street
Woollahra, Sydney 2025
T   9362 1222
E   info@jonesthegrocer.com.au
W   www.jonesthegrocer.com.au

Just William Chocolates [68]
4 William Street
Paddington, Sydney 2021
T   9331 5468
E   info@justwilliam.com.au
W   www.justwilliam.com.au

Kathryn's on Queen [122]
20 Queen Street
Woollahra, Sydney 2025
T/F 9327 4535

E   info@kathryns.com.au
W   www.kathryns.com.au

Ken Done Gallery [20]
1 Hickson Road
The Rocks, Sydney 2000
T   9247 2740
F   9251 4884
E   gallery@done.com.au
W   www.kendonegallery.com

Ken Neale [51]
138 Darlinghurst Road
Darlinghurst, Sydney 2010
T   9331 2033

Koskela Design [58]
Level 1, 91 Campbell Street
Surry Hills, Sydney 2010
T   9280 0999
F   9280 1091
W   www.koskela.com.au

La Buvette [48]
35 Challis Avenue
Potts Point, Sydney 2011
T   9358 5113

La Gerbe d'Or [66]
255 Glenmore Road
Paddington, Sydney 2021
T   9331 1070
W   www.lagerbedor.net

Latteria [51]
320 Victoria Street
Darlinghurst, Sydney 2010
T   9331 2914

Le Kiosk [105]
1 Marine Parade
Manly, Sydney 2095
T   9977 4122
F   9977 3453
E   dining@lekiosk.com.au
W   www.lekiosk.com.au

Leona Edmiston [68]
88 William Street
Paddington, Sydney 2021
T/F 9331 7033
E   paddington@
    leonaedmiston.com.au
W   www.leonaedmiston.com.au

Lisa Ho [70]
2a–6a Queen Street
Woollahra, Sydney 2025
T   9360 2345
W   www.lisaho.com.au

The Loft [154]
3 Lime Street, King Street Wharf
Darling Harbour, Sydney 2000
T   9299 4770
F   9299 4440
E   info@theloftsydney.com
W   www.theloftsydney.com

London Hotel [93]
234 Darling Street
Balmain, Sydney 2041
T   9555 1377

London Tavern [68]
85 Underwood Street
Paddington, Sydney 2021
T   9331 3200

Longrain [137]
85 Commonwealth Street
Surry Hills, Sydney 2010
T   9280 2888
F   9280 2887
E   info@longrain.com
W   www.longrain.com

The Lord Nelson Brewery Hotel [149]
19 Kent Street
The Rocks, Sydney 2000
T   9251 4044
F   9251 1532
E   hotel@lordnelson.com.au
W   www.lordnelson.com.au

Lotus [150]
22 Challis Avenue
Potts Point, Sydney 2011
T   9326 9000
F   9326 9010
E   lotus@merivale.com
W   www.merivale.com

Love & Hatred [33]
Shop 79, Strand Arcade
412–14 George Street
CBD, Sydney 2000
T   9233 3441
E   info@loveandhatred.com.au
W   www.loveandhatred.com.au

Lunch [101]
Shop 5, 100 Edinburgh Road
Castlecrag, Sydney 2068
T   9958 8441

Luxe [33]
Strand Arcade
412–14 George Street
CBD, Sydney 2000
T   9235 2222

Macleay on Manning [47]
85 Macleay Street
Potts Point, Sydney 2011
T   9331 4100

Mambo [166]
17 Oxford Street
Paddington, Sydney 2021
T   9331 8034
F   9331 8035
W   www.mambo.com.au

Manly Ocean Beach House [105]
Ocean Promenade, South Steyne
Manly, Sydney 2095
T   9977 0566
F   9977 0922

Manly Wharf Hotel [147]
Manly Wharf, East Esplanade
Manly, Sydney 2095
T   9977 1266
F   9977 1255
W   www.manlywharfhotel.com.au

Marcs [66]
280 Oxford Street
Paddington, Sydney 2010
T   9332 4255
F   9380 6508
W   www.marcs.com.au

Marque [58]
355 Crown Street
Surry Hills, Sydney 2010
T   9332 2225
F   9332 3090
E   marquerestaurant@bigpond.com
W   www.marquerestaurant.com

Maverick [82]
471 Bronte Road
Bronte, Sydney 2024
T   9388 9068

Medusa [116]
267 Darlinghurst Road
Darlinghurst, Sydney 2010
T   9331 1000
F   9380 6901
E   info@medusa.com.au
W   www.medusa.com.au

The Merchant of Venice [91]
Italian Forum, 23 Norton Street
Leichhardt, Sydney 2040
T   9564 6622

MG Garage [136]
490 Crown Street
Surry Hills, Sydney 2010
T   9360 7007

Michael Hislop [33]
Shop 58-60, Strand Arcade
412-14 George Street
CBD, Sydney 2000
T   9222 9755
W   www.michaelhislop.com

Middle Bar [155]
Kinsela's, 383 Bourke Street
Surry Hills, Sydney 2010
T   9331 6200

Milsons [98]
17 Willoughby Street
Kirribilli, Sydney 2061
T   9955 7075
F   9954 0880
E   info@milsonsrestaurant.com.au
W   www.milsonsrestaurant.com.au

Mimco [66]
436 Oxford Street
Paddington, Sydney 2021
T   9357 6884
W   www.mimco.com.au

Mofo [93]
354 Darling Street
Balmain, Sydney 2041
T   9555 5811

The Monkey Bar [93]
255 Darling Street
Balmain, Sydney 2041
T   9810 1749
E   kay@monkeybar.com.au
W   www.monkeybar.com.au

Moog Hotel [118]
413 Bourke Street
Surry Hills, Sydney 2010
T   8353 8200
E   info@mooghotel.com
W   www.mooghotel.com

Moorish [78]
118-20 Ramsgate Avenue
Bondi, Sydney 2026
T   9300 9511
F   9300 9711
E   info@moorishrestaurant.com.au
W   www.moorishrestaurant.com.au

Morrissey [167]
372 Oxford Street
Paddington, Sydney 2021
T   9380 7422
W   www.oroton.com.au

Mrs Red & Sons [58]
427 Crown Street
Surry Hills, Sydney 2010
T   9310 4860

Mu Shu [82]
108 Campbell Parade
Bondi, Sydney 2026
T   9130 5400

Mura Clay Gallery [88]
49-51 King Street
Newtown, Sydney 2042
T   9550 4433

Museum of Contemporary Art [19]
140 George Street
The Rocks, Sydney 2000

T   9252 4033
F   9252 4361
W   www.mca.com.au

Museum of Sydney [30]
Corner Philip & Bridge Streets
CBD, Sydney 2000
T   9251 5988
E   info@hht.net.au
W   www.hht.nsw.gov.au

Nerida Winter [173]
10/20 Bay Street
Double Bay, Sydney 2028
T   9363 0822

Newtown Old Wares [88]
439 King Street
Newtown, Sydney 2042
T   9519 6705

Nick Brown [57]
397 Bourke Street
Surry Hills, Sydney 2010
T   9360 7334

North Sydney Olympic Pool [98]
Milsons Point, Sydney 2061
T   9955 2309

Norton Street Cinema [91]
99 Norton Street
Leichhardt, Sydney 2040
T   9550 0122

The Nudie House [68]
35 William Street
Paddington, Sydney 2021
T   9332 1388

Object Store [170]
88 George Street
The Rocks, Sydney 2000
T   9247 7984
E   object@object.com.au
W   www.object.com.au

The Observatory Hotel [110]
89-113 Kent Street
The Rocks, Sydney 2000
T   9256 2222
F   9256 2233
E   email@observatoryhotel.com.au
W   www.observatoryhotel.com.au

Oishi [88]
355 King Street
Newtown, Sydney 2042
T   9550 5728
E   oishi@bigpond.com

Old Fitzroy Hotel [45]
129 Dowling Street
Woolloomooloo, Sydney 2011
T   9356 3848
E   manager@oldfitzroy.com.au
W   www.oldfitzroy.com.au

Opal Fields [174]
190 George Street
The Rocks, Sydney 2000
T   9247 6800
W   www.opalfields.com.au

Opium [22]
Level 1, Overseas Passenger Terminal
Circular Quay, Sydney 2000
T   8273 1277
W   www.wildfiresydney.com

Oroton [33]
Shop G24, QVB, 455 George Street
CBD, Sydney 2000
T   9261 1984
W   www.oroton.com.au

Orson & Blake [174]
483 Riley Street
Surry Hills, Sydney 2010

T   8399 2525
83-85 Queen Street
Woollahra, Sydney 2025
T   9326 1155
E   orsonbl@zipworld.com.au
W   www.orsonandblake.com.au

Otto [134]
8, The Wharf
6 Cowper Wharf Road
Woolloomooloo, Sydney 2011
T   9368 7488
F   9360 9688
W   www.otto.net.au

The Oxford [57]
134 Oxford Street
Surry Hills, Sydney 2010
T   9331 3467

Paablo Nevada [70]
1-15 Cross Street
Double Bay, Sydney 2028
T   9362 9455

Paddington Markets [69]
395 Oxford Street
Paddington, Sydney 2021
T   9331 2923
W   www.paddingtonmarket.com.au

Palisade [148]
35 Bettington Street
The Rocks, Sydney 2000
T   9247 2272
F   9247 2040
E   info@palisadehotel.com
W   www.palisadehotel.com

Papaya [162]
15 Transvaal Avenue
Double Bay, Sydney 2028
T   9362 1620
F   9327 2833
E   shop@papaya.net.au
W   www.papaya.com.au

Paul & Joe [66]
222A Glenmore Road
Paddington, Sydney 2010
T   9331 6454
F   9362 9165
W   www.christensen
     copenhagen.com.au

Peel [51]
Shop 2b, 274 Victoria Street
Darlinghurst, Sydney 2010
T   9356 3200

Pentimento [88]
249 King Street
Newtown, Sydney 2042
T   9565 5591

Peter Mitchell Jewellery [102]
23 Pittwater Road
Manly, Sydney 2095
T   9977 3432
F   9907 6596
E   info@petermitchelljewellery.com
W   www.petermitchelljewellery.com

Pier [141]
594 New South Head Road
Rose Bay, Sydney 2029
T   9327 6561
F   9363 0927
E   pierrestaurant@bigpond.com
W   www.pierrestaurant.com.au

Pizza Mario [51]
248 Palmer Street
Darlinghurst, Sydney 2010
T   9332 3320

Planet Furniture [58]
419 Crown Street
Surry Hills, Sydney 2010
T   9698 0680

F   9698 8222
E   enquiries@
     planetfurniture.com.au
W   www.planetfurniture.com.au

Post [31]
Lower Ground Floor, GPO
1 Martin Place
CBD, Sydney 2000
T   9229 7744
E   mail@gposydney.com
W   www.gposydney.com

Powerhouse Museum [37]
500 Harris Street
Ultimo, Sydney 2009
T   9217 0111
F   9217 0333
W   www.phm.gov.au

Pratten [161]
50 William Street
Paddington, Sydney 2021
T   9360 8414
T   9.60 8415
E   justinepratten@bigpond.com
W   www.justinepratten.com

Pretty Dog [90]
1a Brown Street
Newtown, Sydney 2042
T   9519 7839

Prime [31]
Lower Ground Floor, GPO
1 Martin Place
CBD, Sydney 2000
T   9229 7777
E   mail@gposydney.com
W   www.gposydney.com

Providore Pelagio [51]
235 Victoria Street
Darlinghurst, Sydney 2010
T   9360 1011

Pulp [102]
185 Pittwater Road
Manly, Sydney 2095
T   9976 6688

Punch Gallery [93]
209 Darling Street
Balmain, Sydney 2041
T   9810 1014
F   9555 8201
E   info@punchgallery.com.au
W   www.punchgallery.com.au

Quadrivium [33]
Shop 50, QVB, 455 George Street
CBD, Sydney 2000
T   9264 8222
F   9264 8700
E   enquiries@quadrivium.com.au
W   www.quadrivium.com.au

Quarantine Station [105]
North Head Scenic Drive
Manly, Sydney 2095
T   9247 5033
W   www.manlyquarantine.com

Quay [130]
Upper Level, Overseas
Passenger Terminal
Circular Quay, Sydney 2000
T   9251 5600
F   9251 5609
W   www.quay.com.au

R. M. Williams [19]
71 George Street
The Rocks, Sydney 2000
T   9247 0204
F   9247 0207
W   www.rmwilliams.com.au

Ravesi's [124]
118 Campbell Parade

Bondi, Sydney 2026
T 9365 4422
F 9365 1481
E ravesis@bigpond.com.au
W www.ravesis.com.au

Red Leather [51]
298 Palmer Street
Darlinghurst, Sydney 2010
T 9380 8191

Redgum Restaurant Bar [99]
Boronia House, 624 Military Road
Mosman, Sydney 2088
T 9969 8544
F 9969 7544
E enquiries@
redgumrestaurant.com.au
W www.redgumrestaurant.com.au

Regents Court [114]
18 Springfield Avenue
Potts Point, Sydney 2011
T 9358 1533
F 9358 1833
E bookings@regentscourt.com.au
W www.regentscourt.com.au

Remo [165]
98 Brighton Boulevard
Bondi, Sydney 2026
T 9130 2088
F 9130 2188
W www.remogeneralstore.com

Rex Irwin [70]
38 Queen Street, 1st floor
Woollahra, Sydney 2025
T 9363 3212
F 9363 0556
W www.rexirwin.com

Ripples [98]
North Sydney Olympic Pool
Olympic Drive
Milsons Point, Sydney 2061
T 9929 7722

Robyn Cosgrove Rugs [70]
18 Transvaal Avenue
Double Bay, Sydney 2028
T 9328 7692
F 9327 6110
E robyn@
robyncosgroverugs.com.au
W www.robyncosgroverugs.com.au

Rochefort [38]
Ground Floor, 185 Elizabeth Street
CBD, Sydney 2000
T 9264 4408
E info@rochefort.com.au
W www.rochefort.com.au

Rockpool [130]
107 George Street
The Rocks, Sydney 2000
T 9252 1888
F 9252 2421
E enquire@rockpool.com
W www.rockpool.com

Rocks Market [21]
George & Playfair Streets
The Rocks, Sydney 2000
T 9240 8717
W www.therocksmarket.com

RoKit [19]
Argyle Stores, 18–24 Argyle Street
The Rocks, Sydney 2000
T 9247 1332
E rokit@spin.net.au

Rose of Australia Hotel [90]
1 Swanson Street
Erskinville, Sydney 2043
T 9565 1441

**Royal Australian Institute
of Architects** [47]
Tusculum, 3 Manning Street
Potts Point, Sydney 2011
T 9356 2955
F 9368 1164
E nsw@raia.com.au
W www.architecture.com.au

Royal Botanical Gardens [25]
Mrs Macquaries Road
Circular Quay, Sydney 2000
T 9251 8111
F 9251 4403
W www.rbgsyd.gov.au

Royal Hotel [66]
237 Glenmore Road
Paddington, Sydney 2021
T 9331 2604
E enquiries@royalhotel.com.au
W www.royalhotel.com.au

Saba for Men [66]
270 Oxford Street
Paddington, Sydney 2021
T 9331 2685
W www.saba.com.au

**Sailors Thai & Sailors Thai
Canteen** [133]
106 George Street
The Rocks, Sydney 2000
T 9251 2466
F 9251 2610

Salt [135]
Kirketon Hotel
229 Darlinghurst Road
Darlinghurst, Sydney 2010
T 9332 2566
F 9332 2530
E info@saltrestaurant.com.au
W www.saltrestaurant.com.au

Sax Fetish [57]
110a Oxford Street
Surry Hills, Sydney 2010
T 9331 6105
F 9360 3864
E sax@lucreziadesade.com.au
W www.lucreziadesade.com.au

Scanlan & Theodore [66]
443 Oxford Street
Paddington, Sydney 2021
T 9361 6722
W www.scanlanandtheodore.com.au

Sean's Panorama [139]
270 Campbell Parade
Bondi, Sydney 2026
T 9365 4924
F 9130 7843
E panorama@ozemail.com.au
W www.seanspanorama.com.au

Seasalt [82]
1 Donnellan Circuit
Clovelly, Sydney 2031
T 9664 5344
E seasaltcafe@bigpond.com
W www.seasaltcafe.com.au

Sejuiced [82]
487 Bronte Road
Bronte, Sydney 2024
T 9389 9538

Simon Johnson [37/101]
181 Harris Street
Pyrmont, Sydney 2009
T 9552 2522
E pyrmont@simonjohnson.com.au
Shop 6, 100 Edinburgh Road
Castlecrag, Sydney 2075
T 9967 4411
E castlecrag@simonjohnson.com.au
W www.simonjohnson.com

Skipping Girl [81]
124A Roscoe Street
Bondi, Sydney 2026
T 9365 0735
F 9365 0782
E info@skippinggirl.com.au
W www.skippinggirl.com.au

Soho Bar [47]
171 Victoria Street
Potts Point, Sydney 2011
T 9358 6511
E info@sohobar.com.au
W www.sohobar.com.au

Soho Gallery [47]
Corner Crown & Cathedral Streets
Woolloomooloo, Sydney 2010
T 9326 9066
W www.sohogalleries.net

Sosumi [31]
Lower Ground Floor, GPO
1 Martin Place
CBD, Sydney 2000
T 9229 7734
E mail@gposydney.com
W www.gposydney.com

Spacejunk [164]
30 Pittwater Road
Manly, Sydney 2095
T 9976 2944
E shop@spacejunkindustries.com
W www.spacejunkindustries.com

St Mary's Cathedral [38]
St Mary's Road
CBD, Sydney 2000
T 9220 0400
E info@stmaryscathedral.org.au

State Theatre [33]
49 Market Street
CBD, Sydney 2000
T 9373 6852
E admin@statetheatre.com.au
W www.statetheatre.com.au

Strand Hatters [33]
Shop 8, Strand Arcade
412–14 George Street
CBD, Sydney 2000
T 9231 6884
E info@strandhatters.com.au
W www.strandhatters.com.au

The Summit & Orbit [30]
Level 47, Australia Square
264 George Street
CBD, Sydney 2000
T 9247 9777
F 9251 2539
W www.summitrestaurant.com.au

Surfection [105]
82–86 The Corso
Manly, Sydney 2095
T 9977 6955

Suyu Emporium [93]
303 Darling Street
Balmain, Sydney 2041
T 9555 9413

Sweet Art [66]
96 Oxford Street
Paddington, Sydney 2021
T 9361 6617
E sales@sweetart.com.au
W www.sweetart.com.au

Sydney Aquarium [34]
Aquarium Pier
Darling Harbour, Sydney 2000
T 9262 2300
F 9262 2683
W www.sydneyaquarium.com.au

Sydney Fish Market [34]
Corner Pyrmont Bridge Road &
Bank Street
Pyrmont, Sydney 2009
T 9004 1100
W www.sydneyfishmarket.com.au

Sydney Gourmet Burger [91]
172 Norton Street
Leichhardt, Sydney 2040
T 9572 9600

Sydney Opera House [25]
Bennelong Point
Circular Quay, Sydney 2000
T 9250 7777
F 9251 3943
E bookings@sydneyoperahouse.com
W www.sydneyoperahouse.com

Sydney Theatre Company [17]
The Wharf, Pier 4&5,
Hickson Road, Walsh Bay
Millers Point, Sydney 2000
T 9250 1777; restaurant: 9250 1761
F 9247 3584
E mail@sydneytheatre.com.au
W www.sydneytheatre.com.au
22 Hickson Road
Millers Point, Sydney 2000
T 9250 1999
F 9250 1927
W www.sydneytheatre.org.au

Sylvia Chan [68]
20 William Street
Paddington, Sydney 2021
T 9380 5981
W www.sylviachan.com.au

Taka Tea Garden [72]
320 New South Head Road
Double Bay, Sydney 2028
T 9362 1777
F 9362 9777
W www.takateagarden.com.au

TAP Gallery [51]
Level 1, 278 Palmer Street
Darlinghurst, Sydney 2010
T 9361 0440
E tap@acay.com.au
W www.tapgallery.org.au

Taronga Zoo [101]
Bradleys Head Road
Mosman, Sydney 2088
T 9969 2777
W www.zoo.nsw.gov.au

Temple [99]
165 Wycombe Road
Neutral Bay, Sydney 2089
T 9904 0688

Tetsuya's [132]
529 Kent Street
CBD, Sydney 2000
T 9267 2900

thetearoom [33]
Level 3, QVB, 455 George Street
CBD, Sydney 2000
T 9283 7279
F 9283 7276
E info@thetearoom.com.au
W www.thetearoom.com.au

Three Clicks West [142]
127 Booth Street
Annandale, Sydney 2038
T 9660 6652
F 9571 8710
E info@threeclickswest.com.au
W www.threeclickswest.com.au

The Tilbury Hotel [155]
12–18 Nicholson Street
Woolloomooloo, Sydney 2011

T 9368 1955
F 9368 7642
E enquiries@tilburyhotel.com.au
W www.tilburyhotel.com.au

Toby's Estate [47]
129 Cathedral Street
Woolloomooloo, Sydney 2011
T 9358 1196
F 9358 1156
W www.tobysestate.com

Tricketts [126]
270 Glebe Point Road
Glebe, Sydney 2037
T 9552 1141
F 9692 9462
E trickettsbandb@hotmail.com
W www.tricketts.com.au

Trilogie [99]
587 Military Road
Mosman, Sydney 2088
T 9960 7900
W www.trilogie.com.au

Tropicana Caffe [51]
227 Victoria Street
Darlinghurst, Sydney 2010
T 9360 9809
E staff@tropicanacaffe.com
W www.tropicanacaffe.com

T2 [88]
173 King Street
Newtown, Sydney 2042
T 9550 3044
E sales@T2tea.com
W www.T2tea.com

Tuchuzy [78]
90 Gould Street
Bondi, Sydney 2026
T 9365 5371
W www.tuchuzy.com

Tyrone Dearing [47]
12 Macleay Street
Potts Point, Sydney 2011
T 8354 0724
E tdearing@zip.com.au

Uchi Lounge [57]
15 Brisbane Street
Surry Hills, Sydney 2010
T 9261 3524

Ultimo Wine Centre [37]
99 Jones Street
Ultimo, Sydney 2007
T 9211 2380
E info@ultimowinecentre.com.au
W www.ultimowinecentre.com.au

Valhalla [88]
166 Glebe Point Road
Glebe, Sydney 2037
T 9660 8050
W www.valhallacinemas.com.au

Vaucluse House [78]
Wentworth Road
Vaucluse, Sydney 2030
T 9388 7922
W www.hht.nsw.gov.au

Venetia Elaine / Icebirg [81]
71 Hall Street
Bondi, Sydney 2026
T 9665 6855

The Victoria Room [157]
235 Victoria Street, Level 1
Darlinghurst, Sydney 2010
T 9357 4488

Water Bar [153]
W Hotel, Cowper Wharf Road
Woolloomooloo, Sydney 2011

T 9331 9000
W www.starwood.com/whotels

Wayne Cooper [33/66]
Shop 69–71, Strand Arcade
412–14 George Street
CBD, Sydney 2000
T 9221 5292
302 Oxford Street
Paddington, Sydney 2021
T 9332 2940
W www.waynecooper.com.au

The Welcome Hotel [148]
91 Evans Street
Rozelle, Sydney 2039
T 9810 1323
F 9810 4247
E info@thewelcomehotel.com
W www.thewelcomehotel.com

Wheels & Doll Baby [168]
259 Crown Street
Surry Hills, Sydney 2010
T 9361 6244
F 9331 1825
E info@wheelsanddollbaby.com
W www.wheelsanddollbaby.com

White Blue [73]
53 Cross Street
Double Bay, Sydney 2028
T 9327 4015
W www.whiteblue.com.au

WildEast Dreams [91]
102 Norton Street
Leichhardt, Sydney 2040
T 9560 4131
E feast@wildeastdreams.com
W www.wildeastdreams.com

Wildfire & Ember [22]
Ground Level, Overseas Passenger
Terminal
Circular Quay, Sydney 2000
T 8273 1222
F 8273 1223
E info@wildfiresydney.com
W www.wildfiresydney.com

Will & Toby's [51]
Level 1, 292–94 Victoria Street
Darlinghurst, Sydney 2010
T 9356 3255
W www.willandtobys.com.au

**The Yellow Bistro &
Food Store** [48]
57 Macleay Street
Potts Point, Sydney 2011
T 9357 3400

You Never Know [101]
5 Spit Road, shop 3
Mosman, Sydney 2088
T 9968 4911
F 9968 4922
W www.youneverknow.com.au

Yu [47]
171 Victoria Street
Potts Point, Sydney 2011
T 9358 6511
E info@yu.com.au
W www.yu.com.au

Zensation [61]
656 Bourke Street
Redfern, Sydney 2016
T 9319 2788
F 9319 2866
E raydesign@bigpond.com
W www.zensation.com.au

Zimmermann [163]
24 Oxford Street
Woollahra, Sydney 2025

T 9360 5769
W www.zimmermannwear.com

Zink & Sons [57]
56 Oxford Street
Surry Hills, Sydney 2010
T 9331 3675

THE HAWKESBURY RIVER [178]
*Trains from Central Station run to
Brooklyn Station every hour (45
minutes). Riverside Brooklyn
Restaurant is in the marina across
from the station. You can arrange for a
water taxi transfer from here to Oxley's
Boatshed and Peat's Bite, both of
which are water-access only
properties. Alternatively drive over the
Harbour Bridge and take the
Newcastle-bound Freeway 3 to the
bridge over the river and then follow
signs to Brooklyn (1 hour).*

Oxley's Boatshed
c/o Hawkesbury Waterfront Rentals,
PO Box 251
Killara, 2071
T 9985 9888
E info@hawkesburyriver.com
W www.hawkesburyriver.com

Riverside Brooklyn Restaurant
Level 1, Hawkesbury River Marina
Brooklyn, 2083
T 9985 7248

Peats Bite
Box 170
Berowra Heights 2082
T 9985 9040
W www.peatsbite.com

THE HUNTER VALLEY [180]
*The Hunter Valley is 180km northwest
from Sydney (2hrs 30mins). Travelling
north over the Harbour Bridge follow
the signs to Newcastle and Freeway 3.
Remain on the F3 and exit at the
Cessnock signpost. Continue into
Cessnock and follow the signs to
Branxton/Singleton. After passing
Cessnock airport take a left onto Broke
Road and the second left is Halls Road
and the Tower Estate, where you'll also
find Robert's. Tempus Two is nearby.*

Roberts at Pepper Tree
Halls Road
Pokolbin, 2320
T 4998 7330

Tempus Two Winery
Corner Broke & McDonalds Roads,
Pokolbin, 2320
T 4993 3999
W www.tempustwo.com.au
E teamtempus@tempusttwo.com.au

Tower Estate
Corner Halls and Broke Roads
Pokolbin
Hunter Valley, 2320
T 4998 7989
F 4998 7919
E sales@towerestate.com
W www.towerestatewines.com.au

Tower Lodge
Halls Road, Pokolbin
Hunter Valley, 2320
T 4998 7022
E retreat@towerestate.com
W www.towerlodge.com.au

**KATOOMBA, LEURA &
BLACKHEATH** [182]
*Direct trains to Blackheath, stopping
at Leura and Katoomba, leave every
hour from Central Station (2 hours).
Alternatively drive west on Parramatta
Road out of Sydney, taking the Western
Motorway tollway to Strathfield and
then following the Great Western
Highway up into the mountains. Silks
and Vulcans are both within walking
distance of Leura and Blackheath
stations respectively; Echoe's is a
short taxi ride from Katoomba station.*

Silk'sBrasserie
128 The Mall
Leura 2780
T 4784 2534
W www.silksleura.com

Echoes
3 Lilianfels Avenue
Katoomba 2780
T 4782 1966
E enquiries@echoeshotel.com.au
W www.echoeshotel.com.au

Vulcans
33 Govetts Leap Road
Blackheath 2785
T 4787 6899

**PITTWATER, AVALON, NEWPORT,
PALM BEACH** [184]
*If driving, head to Manly then take
Highway 10 north up the coast passing
through Newport and Avalon on the
way to Palm Beach. Or take the ferry
to Manly (30 minutes) from Circular
Quay and then the regular bus up
Highway 10 (45 minutes).*

Swell
Shop 3, 74 Old Barrenjoey Road
Avalon Beach 2107
T 9918 5678

Rockridge
Contemporary Hotels, Beach Houses
& Villas
2/297 Liverpool Street
Darlinghurst, Sydney 2010
T 9331 2881
E info@contemporaryhotels.com.au
W www.beachhousesand
villas.com.au

Jonah's
69 Bynya Road
Palm Beach 2108
T 9974 5599
E jonahs.com.au
W www.jonahs.com.au

Dish
352 Barrenjoey Road
Newport 2106
T 9999 2398
W www.dishnewport.com